PARENTING
WHILE AUTISTIC

Raising Kids When You're Neurodivergent

Wendela Whitcomb Marsh, MA, RSD

Part 4 of the Book Series *Adulting While Autistic*

PARENTING WHILE AUTISTIC
Raising Kids When You're Neurodivergent

All marketing and publishing rights guaranteed to and reserved by:

FUTURE HORIZONS
(817) 277-0727
(817) 277-2270 (fax)
E-mail: info@fhautism.com
www.fhautism.com

Cover and interior by John Yacio III.

ISBN: 9781957984285

Advance Praise for *Parenting While Autistic*

Parenting While Autistic by Wendela Whitcomb Marsh is chock-full of information on autistic considerations through all ages and stages of parenting, from initial planning, pregnancy, and birth all the way through each stage of a child's growing up process, including leaving the nest. Regardless of which stage of parenting you may find yourself in, if you are an autistic parent (or planning to become one), you will want to read this book! Besides the valuable information, each stage of growing up is accompanied by several types of family stories that allow the reader to see how the information presented is implemented in a variety of family configurations and situations. This makes it easy for the reader to imagine forward in their own family, planning implementation of strategies for successful parenting while autistic. Quite valuable!

— Judy Endow, MSW, LCSW, Author, International Presenter,
Mental Health Therapist, Autistic Parent and Grandparent

Praise for Wendela Whitcomb Marsh

Recognizing Autism in Women and Girls: When It Has Been Hidden Well

In the last ten years, we have become increasingly able to identify how autism may be expressed differently in girls and women. This new comprehensive and engaging resource outlines those differences and may encourage parents and autistic adults to seek a diagnostic assessment, which should, in turn, improve the diagnostic abilities of clinicians. The lives of so many girls and women will be transformed by recognition of their autism.

— Professor Tony Attwood, Griffith University, Australia

This book is in memory of

David Scott Marsh,
brilliant and loving autistic dad,

and dedicated to the three
who made us so happy to be parents,

Cat David Robinson Marsh
Siobhan Eleanor Wise Marsh
Noel Maebh Whitcomb Marsh

Contents

Parenting While Autistic

Contents

Parenting While Autistic

Introduction

Family:
Some Assembly Required

"If the day ever came when we were able to accept ourselves and our children exactly as we and they are, then, I believe, we would have come very close to an ultimate understanding of what 'good' parenting means."

— Fred Rogers

Introduction

Some of the best and most caring parents I've known have been autistic. If anyone suggests that autistic people should not have children, in the mistaken belief that they would not be good parents because of their neurodiversity, they are wrong.

Completely wrong.

I have known countless autistic and otherwise neurodivergent (ND) folk who are amazing, loving parents, including the man I married, who fathered our three children as an autistic dad. There is nothing in autism that precludes good parenting.

This is not to say that every autistic person should have a child, any more than every neuro-majority person should. People usually know for themselves whether or not they want to become parents, and if they don't, they shouldn't. It's as simple as that.

But, since you're holding this book right now, I suspect that either you already are a parent or you are considering starting a family. Congratulations! Parenthood is an amazing journey, and speaking for myself, I would not have missed it for the world.

Of course, that doesn't mean that every moment will be sunshine, rainbows, and cute, cuddly babies who sleep all night and never throw their oatmeal at the wall. Babies are just teenagers on hold, and teenagers are adults in waiting. At every step in the growing-up process, there will be hard times, and there will be joyful times. When it comes to families, some assembly is always required. You get to create for yourselves the family you want. If you had great parents, you can emulate them. If your parents made a lot of mistakes, well, now you know what not to do. It's a learning curve, so fasten your seatbelts. But remember: parents have made this same journey since people began peopling, and the journey will continue after our children's children have grandchildren of their own. We're part of a huge spectrum of parenting through the ages. Isn't it a wonder and a privilege to be a link in this chain?

Having a different brain, as autists, ADHDers, and AuDHDers do, does not mean that you shouldn't be part of this link if your heart leads you to parenting. You'll be amazing!

You and I both know, though, that being neurodivergent in a neuro-majority world is not easy. Parenting isn't easy, either. But you can do difficult things. You've been doing them all along, haven't you? Parenting is just one more challenge you can manage, and it's worth it. This book is here to help you navigate the unique aspects of parenting while autistic.

Throughout the book you'll find side trips to focus on various aspects of parenting while autistic. Here's a description of each one.

SENSORY SMARTS

In this section we'll discuss some of the sensory issues related to different stages of the parenting journey. You'll find strategies for coping with your sensory reactions.

MAKE FAMILY MEETINGS FUN

Your family's need for Family Meetings, and what you will focus on in these meetings, will change as your children grow. Keep up with their needs and yours while making it fun for everyone.

Introduction

WEEKENDS THAT WORK

You deserve a break at the end of a busy week, and so do your kids. How can you create the kind of weekend that works for all of you? You'll find tips in this section.

FICTIONAL FAMILIES

Throughout the book, the topics and challenges at your child's developmental stages will be illustrated by fictional families who, like you, are parenting while autistic. Follow them on their journeys, and see what you may have in common with them.

Trish & Bill, Autistic Parents

You may remember Trish and Bill from *Dating While Autistic*, when they first met and fell in love. They showed up again in *Relating While Autistic*, where they got married and navigated a double-neurodivergent relationship. Now, follow them on their parenting journey, from conception through childhood, the teen years, and beyond.

Justin & Maggie, Autistic Dad Adoption Story

Justin and Maggie learned that Justin was autistic in *Relating While Autistic*. In this book we follow them through their struggles with infertility and, eventually, their adoption story.

Parenting While Autistic

Lucia & Naima, Two Autistic Moms

Lucia and Naima met, fell in love, and married in *Relating While Autistic*. The two ND women wanted a family together, and this book shares their unique path to parenthood.

Maria & Santiago, Undiagnosed Autistic Mom

We met Maria in *Independent Living While Autistic: Your Roadmap to Success*, which told of her life as a divorced autistic mother of twin girls who were away at college. In this book we'll learn Maria's backstory with her husband Santiago, beginning even before her twins were born. Find out how Maria dealt with divorce without dividing the family.

Robert & Helen, Grandparenting While Autistic

In *Independent Living While Autistic: Your Roadmap to Success*, we met Robert, who was diagnosed with autism as a retired grandfather, after his grandson was diagnosed. Because their daughter, Lena, and grandson, Bobby, live with them, Robert and his wife, Helen, are involved in Bobby's upbringing as grandparents in residence.

Daisy & Crow, Fur-Baby Parents

Daisy and Crow, who met and fell in love in *Relating While Autistic*, are child-free by choice. They love their fur-baby as deeply as others love their human children. In this book, their child-free decision will be put to the test in an unexpected way. They meet each challenge with humor, and the same daring and courage that helped them

Introduction

defeat the metallic dragons of Uberlon in their legendary D&D campaigns.

PARENT TO PARENT

It's important to listen to the authentic voices of actually autistic parents. Here you will find words of wisdom from neurodivergent moms and dads who have walked the ND parenting path before you and who want you to succeed, too.

You've got this. Let's go.

Chapter 1

Pregnancy & Birth

Coming Soon to a Nursery Near You

"A baby is God's opinion that life should go on."

— Carl Sandburg

1: Pregnancy & Birth

There are those who say you should wait to have a baby until you know you're completely ready, right down to having your child's college fund in the bank. This could cause a couple to wait so long they may miss out on parenting altogether.

Others say you'll never be ready, just go for it now. But this is too important and life-altering a decision to jump straight into without first giving it a good deal of thought and planning.

So when will you know that you are ready?

DIAPERS

One way to address the readiness issue is to think about **DIAPERS**: Desire, Information, Alignment, Planning, Economics, Room, and Support.

Desire
The D in DIAPERS is for Desire.

Do you actually desire a family or are you being pressured to take this step by parents who want grandbabies? Look into your hearts. Spend time with friends and family members who have children of various ages. Sit in a park together and watch the children play, taking note of how their parents interact with them. Would you parent differently if they were your children? How do you really feel about children? Does the idea of holding your own infant bring you joy? What about a toddler, a school-aged child, a teenager, or an adult child who may or may not give you grandchildren of your own? Listen to your heart's desire, and don't be led by others' expectations or societal pressures. After you are clear about your own desire to be parents, it's time to gather information.

Information
The I in DIAPERS is for Information.

Gather as much information about parenting as you can. Look online; read magazines and books about parenting. Talk together about what you have read and learned. What are your responses? Which sources ring true to you, and which should you set aside or ignore? Talk to people you know who have children, and ask them for advice. Would they do things differently today? If you have a counselor, coach, therapist, or doctor you can talk to, ask for their professional opinions and advice. At the end of the day, though, the decision can only be made by the potential parents-to-be. When you have gathered information about parenting, it's important to check and be sure the two of you are in alignment.

Alignment
The A in DIAPERS is for Alignment.

If you will be co-parenting with a spouse or partner, then you need to be aligned with your parenting desire and philosophy. Are the two of you on the same page? It can be difficult for an autistic partner to self-advocate and share how they really feel, especially if they know it is important to their beloved. This is not the time to hold back and let your partner take the lead 100%, though. This decision must be made by both of you together. If you don't want to be a parent but your partner does, you need to be upfront now. If it's too difficult for you to say your truth in person, especially if you're afraid you'll disappoint them, consider writing out your feelings and your reasons behind them. Then find a time when you are both calm and open to communication to share it.

Take an honest look at parenting together. If you're not sure how you feel, then, rather than going along to make your partner happy, you might benefit from short-term couples counseling. You can address your concerns and get clarity about whether you really want to have children but have fear or anxiety about it, or whether you truly do not want to become a parent at all, ever. It is vital to get this answer before going further. You owe it to your partner, yourself, and your potential future family to be sure you're in alignment before going forward on this journey. Once you're in alignment, if it's a yes for both of you, then you can start planning.

Planning
The P in DIAPERS is for Planning.

What could be more important to plan for than parenthood? If you're the kind of autist who loves to have everything organized, this will be right in your wheelhouse. Make lists, charts, spreadsheets, drawings, or whatever you like to do as you plan for parenthood. Many autists have visual strengths, so these representations will be an important part of your planning. If you lean more toward ADHD than OCD, the planning part might not be your strength, but working with your partner to create a plan is a good idea. One important thing to plan for is economics.

Economics
The E in DIAPERS is for Economics.

They say two can live as cheaply as one and that everything is cheaper by the dozen, but nobody ever said that a family of three, four, or a dozen would be without a cost. Start planning out your costs in advance. Do you have medical insurance that covers prenatal examinations, labor, delivery, and neonatal care? What about other costs, such as prenatal vitamins, prepared meals when you're both too tired to cook, diapers, wipes, and all the tiny adorable things babies need?

Make a budget together, and be realistic. If the parent who will be pregnant is working, plan for the time when they will not be able to work. Find out what kind of parental leave your workplaces offer. Take into account that they may need to stop working earlier in the pregnancy than you might think, so plan for the unexpected.

Most people can cut costs when they need to for an important goal, and your new baby is certainly worth making sacrifices for. Now that you're thinking about costs, don't forget to evaluate whether you have room for another family member.

1: Pregnancy & Birth

Room
The R in DIAPERS is for Room.

Babies don't take up a lot of space at first. The things that come with babies do, though. Cribs, dressers, strollers, changing tables, car seats, and mega-packages of diapers and wipes take up a lot of room. If you live in a small one-bedroom, think in advance about where you'll put the crib. Is there room in your bedroom?

What about multi-purposing large items? You can find a dresser that doubles as a changing table, a stroller with a removable car seat, and a crib that will later transform into a toddler bed. Draw a blueprint of your home and decide where everything will go. Not having a big house is no reason not to have a baby, but planning to make room for it in advance is smart.

Once you know you have room, it's not too soon to start thinking about the support you may need.

Support
The S in DIAPERS is for Support.

When there are two parents, they should serve as mutual support for one another. Be sure to have your partner's back, especially if your partner is the one who will be pregnant. That's a huge commitment, and the non-pregnant partner should go above and beyond in the support department, if only because there's no getting around the fact that one partner will be carrying a heavier load, literally.

Look outside your partnership for additional support. Are you connected to any kind of social service system that can offer help, or a counselor? Use any services available; that's what they're there for. Do you have family members who will be happy to step in and help out? Then you are fortunate, indeed. However, do be clear about what kind of help you want and need. If you want someone to come and watch the baby while you nap, let them know. If you'd rather have them do the dishes and laundry while you bond with your new baby, be clear about that, too. If visitors want to come meet the baby, let them know how long you are comfortable with having them stay. When that time is up, graciously thank them for coming and walk them to the door. If they wanted to stay longer, let them know you look forward to their next visit to take the sting out. The bottom line is that you have the right to set boundaries, and others must learn to abide by them.

SENSORY SMARTS

If you've ever been pregnant, whether you're ND or in the neuro-majority, you know there's a lot going on with your senses. Your sense of smell may be heightened so that you are put off by typical odors that didn't bother you before. This affects your appetite, and you may find that there are fewer foods that you can tolerate, despite knowing how important it is to maintain a healthy diet for your baby and for yourself. As you gain weight, which is normal and necessary for a healthy pregnancy, your balance may be affected. You may experience extreme reactions to the feeling of your baby moving within your womb. There is so much going on in your body that there may be times when you don't want to be touched at all, not even by your beloved partner. Don't ignore your sensory responses, but also don't be overly concerned as long as you are under a doctor's care and following their advice. You may need to spend far more time alone in a quiet, darkened room. That's okay.

If you're the non-pregnant partner, it's your job to support your loved one, now more than ever before. Don't judge. Don't minimize their sensory reactions. Do what you can to make this time easier for them and to enjoy the anticipation of your new arrival.

During labor and delivery, there will be even more sensory experiences, and some ND women shut down or dissociate from the overload. Be sure to ask your obstetrician, midwife, doula, and birthing team what to expect. Put plans in writing for what you want regarding pain management and possible interventions if needed. You may need a simple, nonverbal sign to indicate that you have become nonverbal due to sensory overwhelm and that you need them to communicate slowly. Rather than asking you complicated questions requiring a spoken response, they might offer two options and ask you to raise one finger for the first and two fingers for the second. Just because a person has become temporarily nonverbal does not mean that they give up their right to be part of the decisions related to their body and their baby.

Knowing what to expect, that this sensory whirlwind will be temporary, and that the end result is bringing your baby into the world should help ease the overload you may feel.

MAKE FAMILY MEETINGS FUN

Don't wait until you have a teenager to realize you need to touch base and should start having family meetings. It won't go over well. The time to start having family meetings is now.

Your first one, if you haven't already been doing this as a couple, can be your DIAPERS planning meeting. Other family meetings may involve choosing a color scheme for the nursery, researching the best baby car seat, planning your weekends, or reading parenting books and magazines together. Always plan something fun during the meeting, such as a delicious healthy snack, and a favorite activity afterward, such as playing a game together or watching a movie you love. Make it fun for yourselves, not just for the children who will be joining your Family Meetings one day.

WEEKENDS THAT WORK

Everyone needs rest, and when you're pregnant, this is even more important, so plan to rest. You'll need that rest to have strength to plan all the things that need doing before the baby comes.

It's also important to share enjoyable "down time" activities as a couple. If there are things you love to do that you know will be difficult with a baby in tow, plan to do them now. Get out your calendars and look at how many weekends remain until your baby is due. Discount the last few weekends because the baby may decide to come early or the pregnant partner may not feel like being as active.

1: Pregnancy & Birth

Make a list during a family meeting of things you enjoy doing together or things you have wanted to do together but haven't tried yet.

When you have your list, go through it again and mark each item with a dollar sign if it is expensive, or with a "T" if it will take a lot of time. Which ones are "Must Do" activities that you absolutely do not want to miss? Put a star by those. Which ones require advance planning, such as making a reservation or buying tickets? Mark it with a P for Planning. You might include some work activities, such as painting the nursery. Put a W by those that involve work.

Now rank the items based on preference, and start adding them to your calendars. You may not get everything done, but at least you will have made a plan for the weekends you have remaining before the baby comes.

Along with scheduling all those outings you want to go on and activities you want to do, don't forget to plan to rest.

FICTIONAL FAMILIES

Trish & Bill, Autistic Parents

Trish could hardly contain her excitement. She had just read the results of her at-home pregnancy test, and it was clear. She was pregnant! They had just started trying and Trish had assumed it would take a long time, but there it was. Two definite lines on the stick. She looked again to be sure, then put it back in the box and hid it in the back of the under-sink cupboard. She didn't want Bill to find it accidentally; she wanted to tell him herself.

But how, and when?

There were so many things to think about! First, though, was to find an obstetrician. When she'd told her gynecologist that they wanted to start a family, he had been happy for her but let her know she'd need a new OBGYN as he no longer delivered babies. Now she was scrolling through the websites of the doctors he'd recommended, trying to find the one that was right for her. She was so focused she hardly noticed Bill coming in.

"You look so serious. What are you reading?" he asked.

"Hmm. Not reading. Looking for a doctor."

Bill felt his stomach drop. "Are you okay? Let me take you to urgent care," he insisted.

"No, I'm fine, just looking for a new doctor." She continued to scroll, intent on sorting through the websites full of information. There was so much to consider!

"Why?"

"Because mine doesn't deliver." As soon as she said the words, Trish froze for a moment, and then quickly closed her laptop and looked up at Bill. She had blurted it out without planning how she would tell him their good news. This was not how she wanted this to happen.

"Of course he doesn't deliver. He's a doctor, not a pizzeria."

So he didn't get it yet. Could she back out of this and tell him later? She didn't really see how, so she went on.

1: Pregnancy & Birth

"I know. But he doesn't deliver … babies."

"That's no problem. You won't need an obstetrician until … " Bill stopped mid-sentence with his mouth open.

"That's right," she said, trying to judge his response.

"Until you … until we … " Bill was staring at her.

Trish began to worry. Did he get it yet? Was he happy? They had been so excited when they planned to get pregnant, but now that it was a reality, was he having second thoughts?

"Yes," she said.

"So, you're … we're … "

"Yes." The next moment felt like years, but finally Bill's face broke into the biggest grin she'd ever seen.

"We are! We're having a baby?"

"We are!" Trish was laughing and crying at the same time.

Bill pushed aside her laptop and picked her up in a huge hug. Then he put her down and looked as if he was afraid he'd broken her. "Are you all right?"

She nodded. "Perfectly all right." He hugged her again, and she realized that he was crying, too. The two of them stood for a long time in each other's arms.

The months to come were busy ones for the parents-to-be. They told their families and friends and found a new doctor who delivers. Trish informed the university that she would be taking maternity leave. They made a sensory plan for Trish to try to predict and alleviate potential overwhelming but unavoidable situations during labor and birth. They planned to go to one more *Star Trek* convention as a couple during the first trimester. On weekends they worked at turning the spare room into a nursery. The next nine months were going to be an adventure. Sometimes adventures are precarious and uncomfortable, but Trish and Bill were prepared to go forth boldly, side by side and hand in hand.

Justin & Maggie, Autistic Dad Adoption Story

Justin and Maggie had been trying to get pregnant for over a year. She was tired of the feeling of failure each time she got her period. He was heartbroken to see the look on her face every time she told him.

Finally, they decided at a family meeting to talk to a fertility doctor. They both got tested and learned that each of them had conditions that contributed to infertility. She had a history of uterine fibroids, and he had a low sperm count and low testosterone. It was difficult news to hear. Justin wondered if it was somehow his fault, maybe because he was autistic. The doctor reassured them that there was no correlation between autism and infertility and that it wasn't anyone's fault. The good news: now that they knew, they could explore other options for parenthood.

After learning a lot about in vitro fertilization, artificial insemination, and adoption, Justin and Maggie finally decided that adoption was the best choice for them. They wanted to open their home to a child who needed them rather than going to extreme lengths to get pregnant themselves. They realized that adoption wasn't a quick or easy process, either, but they were sure. Maggie's mother was adopted, so they had a positive support person already in their corner. Justin wanted to make Maggie happy, and the more he thought about it, the stronger he felt about adoption. He hadn't admitted it to Maggie, but he had been secretly terrified at the thought of her going through the pain of labor. As much as he wanted to be there for her, just imagining her in pain and fearing that she could die in childbirth had been devastating for him. Adoption was the perfect choice.

Lucia & Naima, Two Autistic Moms

Lucia and Naima knew they were ready to start a family together. They had planned and dreamed, and now it was time to take the next step. But which of them would be the one to carry their baby? They wanted the traditional experience of pregnancy that most couples share, so adoption was not on the table for them. But how to decide? Each of them would be happy to be pregnant and equally happy to support the other in pregnancy. They both felt healthy and strong enough. Finally, they decided to let their doctor guide them.

After each of them had a full physical exam and medical history, they sat down in their doctor's office together to hear her recommendation. The doctor told them they were both healthy enough to conceive and carry a child to term with no foreseen difficulties, so it was difficult to make a recommendation. However, in reviewing their history, she noted that Naima's mother had experienced gestational diabetes during each of her pregnancies and had gone on to develop type 2 diabetes in middle age. Because of this, she recommended that Lucia be the one to carry their child.

They thought about this advice and decided to take it. Lucia would become pregnant with their child, through artificial insemination.

They did a lot of research into the pros and cons of the various types of artificial insemination, guided by the specialist their doctor had recommended. They wondered about anonymous donors and thought about what their baby might inherit from a stranger, good or bad. There was no way of knowing, but they knew of no other way.

Then a wonderful thing happened at Naima's birthday party. Their families gathered to enjoy her favorite macaroni and cheese, Cajun-spiced collard greens, and her mom's original recipe for sweet potato cake. Then Naima's brother had an announcement. As his birthday present to his sister, he offered to be their sperm donor. That way their baby would have DNA from both Lucia's and Naima's families. Everyone started crying and hugging. Later they would put her brother in touch with their fertility doctor to begin the arrangements, but for tonight, it was a time for celebration.

Maria & Santiago, Undiagnosed Autistic Mom

Maria met Santiago in high school. No one else had really paid attention to her, and she was so shy that it was easy for her to disappear. But Santiago noticed her. He seemed to like her, which came as a surprise. At first, she was very nervous around him, but

1: Pregnancy & Birth

in time he won her over. She found him charming, and he pursued her with patience but persistence. It was difficult for her to say no to him, which is how she found herself pregnant in the spring of their senior year in high school. She had always been a good Catholic girl and was terrified of her parents and the holy sisters discovering her sin. Santiago offered to marry her quickly and quietly. By the time her pregnancy was apparent, they were already newlyweds living with his parents. Soon he got a job, and they got their own apartment.

Maria had led a sheltered life and her mother never talked about pregnancy and birth, so she didn't have a clear idea of what to expect. She knew women had always gone through it, so she would, too, but her prenatal education and care was minimal. She found it stressful to make phone calls and arrange doctor's appointments, and Santiago didn't seem to care if she went to a doctor or not.

When she went into labor, the sensory experience was so intense that she shut down and had very little memory of any of it. Apparently there was some kind of complication, so she had a C-section under general anesthesia. When she woke up, she was told that she had healthy twin girls. Surprise! Also, her mother informed her that Santiago had gone out to celebrate with his friends. Not a surprise.

As soon as she looked into the two tiny faces of her daughters, Maria didn't care about the pain or Santiago's lack of support. Her entire world now would be these two perfect little girls.

Parenting While Autistic

Although she lacked experience, she knew her mission in life was to become the best mother she could possibly be for them. They deserved no less.

Robert & Helen, Grandparenting While Autistic

Robert didn't choose retirement, but it seemed the world had no place for an old-fashioned television repairman. Being at home was hard on him and on his wife, Helen. When they got the news that their daughter, Lena, was pregnant and needed to move in with them, it turned out to be the best news ever. It didn't take long for Robert and Helen to get over the shock of their daughter being a single mother and to embrace their new roles as grandparents. Back then, no one knew that their grandson, Bobby, would be diagnosed with autism, or that Robert would also be found to be autistic. The world now revolved around supporting Lena and getting ready for their grand baby. Retirement was starting to look like a lot more fun.

Daisy & Crow, Fur-Baby Parents

(Daisy and Crow sit on the couch. She holds their new puppy, a brown and white mix of something fluffy and something scruffy. Crow sketches a picture of the two of them.)

CROW: What do we call him? We can't keep saying, "The Baby."

DAISY: I've been thinking about that. Should we name him after the dwarf, Aaravocra the Avenger?

CROW: Too hard to pronounce. Goblin?

1: Pregnancy & Birth

DAISY: He does gobble, but no, too Halloweeny. FluffyKiller?

CROW: He's certainly fluffy. But what about Erymindor Longtail?

DAISY: A serious name for such a little cutie patootie. What about Truly Scrumptious?

CROW: Never!

DAISY: Too gender-specific? With one nonbinary parent, I guess we should keep it neutral. He's just such an adorable little bugbear!

CROW: I think you've got it!

DAISY: Got what?

CROW: *(rises, drawing pencil still in hand)* Good mutt. I dub thee Sir BugBear! *(gently touches each of his furry shoulders with the pencil)* Arise, knight of the Crow and Daisy Family, and accept your place in our Forever Home.

DAISY: It's perfect! BugBear, you are such a precious little fluffer-muffin!

CROW: *(pauses, watches Daisy and BugBear being adorable together)* So tell me, have you ever thought about … you know …

DAISY: I know many things, but what you're thinking right now is not one of them.

CROW: You know, having a baby?

DAISY: Like, a human baby?

CROW: Yeah, that's what people usually mean when they say baby. A human one.

DAISY: Me? No way! I mean—wait, did you want to have one of those? Please say it ain't so, Crow!

CROW: God, no! I just didn't want you to miss out if you really wanted to. A lot of people seem to like it. Thought I'd ask, is all.

DAISY: I have thought about it, and there is no way I will ever want to be a parent. Ever. It is not my path. This little bundle of adorableness is the only baby I need or want.

CROW: *(sighs)* That is such a relief. I didn't want to stand in your way if you wanted to be a mother—of a human—but I can't see myself as a parent, either.

DAISY: Let's make a pact between us: no human progeny, only fur babies!

CROW: *(chants with her)* No human progeny, only fur babies!

(Little did they know the unexpected twists and turns their lives would take and how dramatically their little family would change. Isn't life full of wonderful surprises?)

PARENT TO PARENT

"When I was born in 1961, we did not have the term autism spectrum disorder. I was very inquisitive and very particular in my communication. When I married my childhood sweetheart, we decided that we were not going to have children. I was busy pursuing my acting career, and we enjoyed our time together so much. Also, I didn't feel that I had the temperament that would be good for raising kids. I grew up learning abuse, and that's all I knew about raising children. But as fate would have it, we got

1: Pregnancy & Birth

pregnant a few months after getting married. After crying for three days, I enrolled myself in therapy. I went in and sat down and said, 'I don't know how to raise kids. I just know abuse, and I need to learn a new way.' My goal was to become a perfect dad. That began my several decades of interaction with therapy, which continues to this day."

— James, late-diagnosed autistic dad

"I have three daughters, and with each, I had very different birth experiences: I had my first daughter at age twenty-eight in a homebirth but ended up transferring to a hospital after I suffered a rare complication.

"During my pregnancy, I had read a lot about how important bonding with your infant was, so when I got to the hospital and they tried to take my several-hours-old baby from me so I could recover, I objected so strongly that they had no choice but to assign a nurse to hold the baby while sitting next to me. For this, I truly credit my autistic traits of locking into one idea, and an indifference to certain social norms. At that point, my only goal was giving my daughter the best start in life possible, and I used my 'stubbornness' to advocate for her.

"Because of the rare complication I experienced with my first daughter, my second daughter was born in a hospital and, while not quite as great as a homebirth, [it] was still a good experience. I found my tunnel vision and laser focus to be extremely valuable during the birthing process, as I could focus on the sensations in my

Parenting While Autistic

body and treat them as 'intense' rather than 'painful.' This focus also allowed me to tune out some of the over-stimulating environment of the hospital, such as the bright lights and noises.

"My third daughter, born ten years after her sisters, was born at home in a wonderful home birth experience that was incredibly positive. My midwives were very supportive of everything I needed for an ideal environment for focusing—they spoke softly, only came in the room when I called them, and didn't get anxious about my desire to birth almost entirely alone. They were also very helpful in providing images I could use as I focused on the contractions, and they encouraged me to labor in water, which I found very calming.

"I think the most important thing with birth and being autistic is to figure out how you focus best and what kind of environment you need for doing something as intense and challenging like birth. Do you need low lights? No noise? Fewer/no people? Personally, I found home birth much more suited to my needs because I could adjust anything and everything in the environment, whereas in the hospital there was a lot of sensory stimulation over which I had no control. My sensitivity also gave me a distinct advantage during the birthing process, as I could more easily describe sensations to my midwives.

"Birth is a truly amazing experience, and my autism allowed me to experience it on what might be a deeper and more profound level."

— Krista, autistic mom

Chapter 2

Newborn & Infancy

"Help" is a Complete Sentence

"Babies are such a nice way to start people."

— Don Herold

"People who say they sleep like a baby usually don't have one."

— Leo J. Burke

2: Newborn & Infancy

I f this is your first child, congratulations! If it's your second child, middle child, or last child, congratulations to you, too! Every new baby is a big change, and your life will not be the same. If this has been difficult for you, it's a good time to learn to ask for help. It's not always easy to admit that we can't do it all, but this is the time to ask for, and accept, the help you need and deserve.

You are embarking on a journey which will be filled with awe-inspiring joy and wonder, as well as incredibly stressful challenges, which may be intensified by your autism. A solution is to try to predict what will be most difficult for you and put plans in place to alleviate the potential problems.

NAPTIME

One way to do this is to remember the word **NAPTIME**. Not just because naptime is a great time for you to relax and temporarily escape the constant pulls of parenting, but also because of what it stands for: Needs, Assets, Planning, Treat, Interventions, Mothers-in-law, Energy conservation. NAPTIME.

Needs
The N in NAPTIME is for Needs.

Needs assessment is an important first step in preparing for the demands of parenting an infant. What do you anticipate will be the most difficult for you? Social events like christenings, or introducing your new baby to groups of friends and family gatherings?

Parenting While Autistic

Sensory experiences like breastfeeding? Regulation issues like lack of sleep and changes to routine? Physical or hormonal changes? Knowing what you are most likely to need will help you alleviate these challenges when they occur.

Assets

The A in NAPTIME is for Assets.

Available assets can help you with the needs you've identified. If you're fortunate enough to have financial assets at your disposal, you will have the option of hiring help, such as a housekeeper or nanny. You may have someone else prepare or deliver meals, and you might opt for a diaper delivery service.

Not everyone has financial assets at their disposal, though. Many other kinds of assets can be even more valuable to you.

Your partner is usually your most important asset. They might notice when you are exhausted, or when you are approaching sensory overload, and step in to take on their share of the parenting load. Remember that the non-pregnant parent, or a parent who works outside the home, is also a full-time parent, 100%, and not a babysitter or helper. If you're the non-child-bearing parent, notice how you step into your parenting role. Offering to help and asking what you can do sounds nice, but remember—your partner didn't magically become all-knowing by giving birth. You are both learning about parenting on this journey together, as equal partners. You can probably figure out what needs to go into the diaper bag if you're going out with the baby, and take care of packing it yourself

2: Newborn & Infancy

rather than asking what you should do. Constant questions can be stressful, and "Assistant Parent" is not a thing. Step up and be the asset your partner needs.

Other family members, friends, and support networks can also be your assets. Look around and see who and what in your life can help you with your identified needs.

Planning

The P in NAPTIME is for Planning.

Planning ahead makes even the most unforeseeable adventure feel a bit more manageable.

If you know that social events will be difficult for you, try the **DEAR** plan: **Decline** as many invitations as you can, have your **Exit** strategy in place before you arrive, **Advocate** for your needs, and plan to **Rest** and recover after it's over.

If your responses to sensory experiences are difficult in the best of times, plan ahead to avoid meltdowns. Nursing may be challenging for you. Consider enlisting the support of a lactation specialist if you choose to breastfeed. Search online for "lactation consultant, autism" in your area. If you have talked to your pediatrician and explored the options and decide to bottle-feed, don't second guess your decision or let anyone try to shame you for your choice. No matter what you've been told, fed is best. You do what is right for you and your baby.

What are the warning signs that you are at risk for losing control due to sensory overwhelm? Know what the signs feel like to you, and what they look like to your partner, so you will be able to make a change before it's too late.

If regulation is a problem for you, plan ways to cope with the dysregulation that is part of life with a newborn. People will tell you to sleep when your baby naps, and that might be the right thing for you, but maybe you'd cope better if you engage in a special interest or play a favorite game while the baby naps. Think about what it is for you that recharges your battery when you need to be replenished. Lying in a dark room listening to your playlist on headphones? Getting out in nature? Being alone with a pet? Plan to do the things that help you to regulate your system when the world feels out of control.

Also, plan to talk to your doctor about what to expect physically after your baby is born. If you're the pregnant parent, find out about hormone ups and downs and what you might do to assist in recovery during the post-natal period.

Treat

The T in NAPTIME is for Treat.

Treat yourself whenever you can. Parenting is exhausting for both of you, and you deserve to carve out time to pamper and take care of yourselves and each other. It might mean preparing or bringing in your partner's favorite food. It might mean settling in on a couch full of fluffy cushions and re-watching your favorite movie while the baby sleeps. It might be taking or finding online a picture of something beautiful or something related to your partner's passions and interests and sending them a text with the image. Whatever feels special to you, when you find a moment to yourselves, indulge and treat yourselves with it.

Interventions
The I in NAPTIME is for Interventions.

Interventions may be necessary if either one of you approaches a meltdown situation. If you see the warning signs that your partner is heading for sensory or social overload, such as noticing their face becoming pinker, their breathing becoming more rapid, or their ability to speak decreasing, you might need to intervene. Take the baby and send your spouse to their favorite recovery place for a calming activity or just a quiet lie-down. They may not be aware of the oncoming meltdown until it's too late, so a loving intervention from their partner may be just what they need.

Conversely, if you are feeling stressed and anxious, and your partner steps in and says, "Go lie down, put on your headphones, take a break," listen to them. Accept the intervention. You know you'd do the same for them if they were the one feeling overwhelmed. Co-parents have each other's backs.

Mothers-in-Law
The M in NAPTIME is for Mothers-in-law.

Mothers and mothers-in-law make great support people and babysitters. (So do fathers and fathers-in-law, but 'Mothers' starts with an M, and NAPTIFE isn't a word.) Aunts, uncles, siblings, and friends are also excellent sources of support. Choose wisely, though. If you have someone in your life who is a critic rather than a cheerleader, you may need to limit your time with them when you're in a vulnerable state. Except overly critical or toxic people, most grandparents have a deep and abiding love for your baby and can be excellent sources of support, especially during the newborn months when you're still recovering from pregnancy, labor, and birth.

Energy

The E in NAPTIME is for Energy.

Energy conservation is vital during the first year of your baby's life and beyond. Recognize your need for recovery after stressful experiences, and plan time to recuperate after social and sensory challenges. Rest is not a luxury or an option; it is a necessity that should not be ignored.

SENSORY SMARTS

There are ways that parenting a newborn can overwhelm the senses. Tactile sensitive people can become overwhelmed by the constant contact of life with an infant. If you're overly bothered by the feeling of tiny nails on your skin and worried about your baby accidentally scratching their own face, you can find shirts and sleepers with fold-over "mittens" so you can sometimes cover their hands with soft cotton. If breastfeeding is too much tactile input, consult a lactation specialist. Not everyone is able to breastfeed or chooses to, so feel free to talk to your pediatrician about the best alternative for feeding your baby. Choose what's right for you, and don't listen to anyone who tries to make you feel bad or talk you out of your choice. It is your body.

If you are soothed by regular movement, you may find that rocking your baby to sleep is just as important to you as it is for your little one. The gentle swaying is relaxing and can provide a much-needed respite from the busy day for both of you.

Changing diapers is not a pleasant task for anyone, but it can be particularly difficult for a parent who has extreme olfactory avoidance. Consider wearing a swimmer's nose plug for the task or a face mask with a drop or two of your favorite scent, extract or perfume on it—something strong enough to do the job. If you're less bothered by smells than your partner is, it would be a great kindness if you offer to do more than your share of the diaper changes.

Once you start spoon-feeding your baby soft foods, if you find that you cannot abide the smell of spinach baby food, choose types with a weaker aroma. Your baby can still get their nutritional needs met without spinach, and you can enjoy feeding time more.

MAKE FAMILY MEETINGS FUN

Your infant will not need to attend family meetings, and you may not feel the need to have them as frequently, but don't give up the practice of sitting down together. Having a special time set aside for face-to-face communication is important, even if you're just coordinating who takes the baby to which well-baby checkups. Your relationship is worth the time to devote to each other, even if it's brief and rare. Keep those meetings on the calendar, whether they're weekly, monthly, or quarterly. If you haven't given them up completely, it will be easier to increase frequency later when you have more time.

WEEKENDS THAT WORK

Don't feel the need to spend your weekends doing a lot of housework and yardwork. You have a new baby now. When you're not working, plan to spend time just hanging out with the baby and each other, and enjoying your new little family. The housework can wait, or you can ask a helpful family member or friend to pitch in. You may have to work during the week, but give yourself the weekend luxury of enjoying your child's babyhood when you can.

FICTIONAL FAMILIES

Trish & Bill, Autistic Parents

It's a boy! Trish and Bill were thrilled to welcome a son into their arms and home.

The labor and delivery had been difficult for Trish, even though she had learned all she could in advance about what to expect. Having Bill at her side made it manageable for her. He was her

2: Newborn & Infancy

anchor, and she was grateful to have him at her side. She needed his hand to squeeze, his soft, loving words in her ear reminding her that a contraction would soon be over.

Bill had thrown himself into learning all he could about labor so that he could be the best labor coach he could be. Trish deserved no less. For his own comfort, he wore a gold and black Star Trek uniform shirt during the birth, not caring what the doctors and nurses thought. Seeing him in it reminded Trish of how they met and of their shared love of science fiction history.

She was overwhelmed by the extreme sensory experience of giving birth and felt as if she were dissociating at times, out of touch with what was going on around her. Later, she couldn't remember all of the labor and delivery process, but she would never forget the moment when they placed her baby in her arms. Bill was at her side to welcome their baby, James. Trish was relieved that they had a boy. She loved the name James, which was her grandfather's middle name, but their private and primary reason for choosing the name was for Captain James T. Kirk of the Starship *Enterprise*. Had their baby been a girl, Bill wanted to name her Uhura after Kirk's communications officer. Trish hated to disappoint him, but she didn't want to be guilty of cultural appropriation, naming a white baby after an iconic African American science fiction legend. Thank goodness for baby James! With him in her arms and Bill at her side, she felt their family was complete.

Parenting While Autistic

Justin & Maggie, Autistic Dad Adoption Story

Justin and Maggie had hoped to adopt an infant, but they soon realized that the adoption process and wait time for an infant was much longer than they expected. Years longer. They had already completed all of the required paperwork, background checks, inspections, and interviews. All that was left was the waiting.

Waiting was hard. Justin had always found the unknown to be especially difficult to deal with, and he had learned this was probably part of his autism. Not knowing what to expect was the worst. Would they have a boy or a girl? From the US or another country? And when would they know? It was hard on both of them, but Justin had more difficulty managing the stress. At least Maggie now understood since he had gotten his diagnosis and they had learned so much about autism. When he got cranky or irritable, rather than snapping back at him and getting into an argument, she simply put her arms around him and held him without saying a word. It was the best way to help him get through the difficult times of uncertainty.

Finally, after not hearing a word for several weeks, they got a call from their adoption case manager. Maggie took the call. She put it on speaker so Justin could hear it all without needing to talk on the phone himself, since that was stressful for him.

"Is our baby being born?" Maggie was breathless with excitement. They had waited so long for this call, her words came tumbling out. "When? Where? We can get on a plane today! We'll be there as soon as he's ready to come home from the hospital. Or she. Do we know yet?"

2: Newborn & Infancy

"It's a boy, but he's not being born today."

"Tomorrow? Is his mother in labor yet?"

"Actually, he was born two years ago. That's what I wanted to talk to you about."

Maggie was silent. "Two years ago?"

"Yes. I know he's older than you expected, but he needs a home, a family. And I think you two would be perfect for him."

Maggie looked at Justin, and he shrugged. They were both processing this in their own ways, and he wasn't ready to talk yet.

"Can you tell me why he's being put up for adoption now instead of two years ago? And where has he been all this time, in an orphanage or something?"

"He's been living with his mother. Although she was a very young teen when she got pregnant, she wanted to keep her baby. Unfortunately, there were some complications that she just isn't equipped to handle, so she made the difficult choice to let him be adopted by a family who can meet his unique needs."

"What do you mean, unique needs?"

"He has a very rare syndrome. It can have a number of possible challenges, including intellectual disability and autistic-like behaviors and responses."

Justin spoke up for the first time. "He's autistic?"

"He doesn't have that diagnosis at this time, but he can be expected to present similar symptoms. As he grows and develops, his medical and educational teams will know more, but right now he's just a very little boy who needs loving parents."

"Yes!" Justin blurted out. "Yes! I mean—" He looked at Maggie. "I mean, we'll have to talk about it, of course …"

"No," said Maggie.

Justin's face fell. "No?"

"No, we don't have to talk about it." Her eyes were brimming with tears. "Yes! Yes, we want to adopt him."

"Are you sure?"

They looked at one another, and they both knew. This was their child, meant to be part of their family.

"We're sure," Maggie said. "So when do we get to meet him?"

Lucia & Naima, Two Autistic Moms

Lucia's labor and delivery went comparatively smoothly, largely because of the tremendous amount of planning and preparation they put into it. They worked with a midwife and doula in a birthing center attached to their local hospital, so if there had been complications, they could easily have had access to medical services. Because the midwife had two autistic children of her own, she understood about sensory overload and communication regression during times of extreme stress. It made all the difference!

Lucia and Naima were side by side when they welcomed their daughter into the world. She was so very precious. In fact, they named her Precious. No other name came close to their feelings about her. Precious Ruby, after Naima's grandmother, Ruby.

After Precious was born, their large families were anxious to meet her. Everyone wanted to come to the house. It was difficult for

2: Newborn & Infancy

either Lucia or Naima to say no to their families, especially when so much love was being beamed in their direction. Unfortunately, Lucia was too exhausted to cope. The sensory overload of recovering from the birth plus learning to breastfeed was enough. She could not deal with social overload on top of it.

For the first visit, Naima tucked Lucia into bed and brought the baby into the living room to meet her grandparents, who arrived masked and prepared for a short visit. Each of them got to hold Precious briefly, and Naima got pictures of them before ushering them back out and bringing Precious back to Lucia.

Later, more family members wanted to visit or invite them to parties, and they didn't feel like they could keep turning everyone down. Finally, they decided on a DEAR plan: Decline, Exit strategy, Accommodations, and Recovery.

Decline: They politely turned down invitations to bring the baby to parties or church. Since Precious was too young to be vaccinated, it made sense that they would not allow her to be in crowds.

Exit strategy: When they did allow family members and friends to come in small groups, wearing masks, the invitation included an end time. When that time came, Naima stood up, thanked them for coming, got their coats and bags, and stood by the open door. No one missed their cue to say goodbye and leave the new little family in peace. It was hard for Naima at first, because she loved their families and would never want to hurt anyone's feelings. She created a script for herself and mentally rehearsed what she would say and do when it was time for their

Parenting While Autistic

guests to leave. Planning it out in advance made it easier for her to implement their exit plan.

Accommodations: Lucia and Naima talked about what accommodations would help Lucia tolerate having people in their house. She was a private person and their home was her refuge, so she was never comfortable with company. The sound of the doorbell triggered her anxiety every time. They decided to tell everyone to text when they got to the house instead of ringing the doorbell or knocking. People might assume it was to avoid waking the baby, but it was really Lucia who needed that accommodation. Another accommodation was that when people arrived, she would be seated in the corner of the couch, surrounded by cushions and pillows like in a nest. The position was comforting to her. Precious would be in her arms, and the baby seat would be on the couch beside her so that no one could sit too close. Knowing they had an exit plan helped her tolerate the social events that seemed inevitable with a new baby.

Recovery: The most important part of the event for Lucia was the planned recovery time after each visit. She needed at least two days with nothing at all planned, no well-baby check-ups, no family members dropping by, nothing. They both needed this. Although Naima wasn't nursing or recovering from childbirth, the emotionally overwhelming change of becoming a parent was new to her. Navigating anything new was exhausting.

Both moms agreed that Precious was worth anything and everything. They already couldn't imagine their lives without her.

2: Newborn & Infancy

Maria & Santiago, Undiagnosed Autistic Mom

Caring for twins as an inexperienced teenager was terribly difficult for Maria, and Santiago offered very little support. Maria's mother, Graciela, helped her make the well-baby appointments and got them all to the doctor's visits on time, knowing that talking with strangers and organizing had always been difficult for her daughter. No one realized that Maria was autistic, but those who were closest to her knew that there were some things that she needed help with. When Graciela saw how overwhelmed Maria was and how little help she got from Santiago, she moved in with them for the twins' first few months of life. The apartment was small, so she took charge and told Santiago he would be sleeping on the couch, while she shared the bedroom with her daughter and granddaughters. Santiago was in the habit of coming home late after drinking with his buddies after work, and she would not have him disturbing Maria's rest or waking the babies. She also worried about Maria's health and ability to cope if she were to become pregnant again too soon after the twins were born. Graciela would be the gatekeeper, whose primary job was keeping Santiago from further disrupting her daughter's life.

Maria was deeply grateful for her mother's presence as she learned how to be a good mother to her new twins. She found that she didn't miss Santiago, even as he started coming home later and less frequently. Her focus was on her daughters, Faith and Hope. They were her life now.

Parenting While Autistic

Robert & Helen, Grandparenting While Autistic

After Lena moved in and before her baby was born, Robert felt completely out of the loop. Helen was so much better at all that than he had ever been. When Lena was born, he had been out in the waiting room with a pocket full of cigars to hand out and had no part in the labor or delivery. He understood things were different now, as Helen took on the role of labor coach for Lena. It left Robert feeling a little left out, but he certainly didn't want to get involved with all that female stuff. He spent most of his time puttering around with his collection of cathode ray tubes, sorting and organizing them again and again. It gave him peace in a household full of womenfolk.

When Lena went into labor, he once more found himself consigned to the waiting room. There were no other dads there, only grandparents. He chatted a bit with the guys, but mostly he flipped through magazines and paced. He developed a regular pacing pattern during the hours he was there: over to the window, then down the hall to look at the vending machine (nothing had changed there since the previous seven trips), then down the hall the other way to look out that window, then back to his seat. Same pattern every time. Robert had never heard of autism at that point; he just knew that walking in the exact same pattern again and again helped him feel better.

Finally, a nurse came to tell him the news: he had a grandson! Robert couldn't have been happier or prouder, or so he thought. Later, when Lena told him she was naming her son Robert, Bobby

2: Newborn & Infancy

for short, his heart was fit to burst out through his chest. He didn't have words, but he hoped Lena and Helen understood how he felt anyway. They usually did.

Daisy & Crow, Fur-Baby Parents

(Daisy and Crow are standing outside the comic book store after a D&D session with their friend Kitty, a fourteen-year-old trans girl assigned male at birth (AMAB). Kitty is holding Bugbear, who is delighted.)

DAISY: Thanks for helping us entertain Bugbear during the game, Kevin. I mean Kitty! I'm so sorry!

KITTY: That's okay. I know it's hard to get used to. At least you're trying to get it right.

CROW: I would hope everyone who knows you would be trying. It wasn't easy for me to come out as nonbinary, and I'd guess it's harder for people to get used to you being trans. But everyone will get used to it.

KITTY: I wish. *(buries her head against Bugbear's fur)*

DAISY: Is anyone in the game giving you a hard time? Tell me who; I'll have a talk with them. With my Sword of Vengeance!

CROW: Seriously, Kitty, let us help.

KITTY: Well, do you think I could come over to your house for a while? I don't want to go home until my dad's asleep.

DAISY: Of course!

CROW: How's your dad taking it, your being Kitty now?

KITTY: Not great. I'm not turning out to be the son he always wanted.

DAISY: But you're the perfect daughter. He'll get used to it.

KITTY: I'm not so sure. But thanks for letting me hang out with you guys tonight.

CROW: Anytime. We're your friends.

DAISY: That's right. Mi castle es su castle.

CROW: I don't think that's how the saying goes ...

DAISY: *(smiles)* It is now.

PARENT TO PARENT

"Because of my determination to be the perfect dad, the first thing I did was go out and buy a book describing the first twelve months of a child's life (e.g., *The First Twelve Months of Life: Your Baby's Growth Month by Month*, by Frank Caplan and Theresa Caplan). I read each chapter diligently prior to that month, so when things happened as they were supposed to, I was prepared with my studies."

— James, late-diagnosed autistic dad

"Because I was diagnosed after my children were older, I really didn't understand that I needed recovery time when my children were infants. If I had it to do over again, I would have created better support systems for myself that included childcare so that I could get regular breaks. At the time, I had one day per week of childcare by a family member so that I could work. My husband had a very demanding job, so a lot of the daily childcare fell to me. I found the

2: Newborn & Infancy

24/7 nature of infant care somewhat overwhelming, and I think that experience would have been much different if I had had more childcare support."

— Krista, autistic mom

Chapter 3

Toddlers & Preschoolers

Now They're Mobile

"Tantrums are not bad behavior.

Tantrums are an expression of emotion that became too much for the child to bear.

No punishment is required.

What your child needs is compassion and safe, loving arms to unload in."

— Rebecca Eanes, *The Newbie's Guide to Positive Parenting*

3: Toddlers & Preschoolers

Parenting toddlers is hard work for anyone. When either the parents or the toddlers are autistic, it is more complicated. When both are, that can certainly add to the challenges. At the same time, though, having a parent who understands autism is a particular and unique gift for an autistic toddler.

UNWANTED ADVICE

Everyone you know seems to have parenting advice. It's easy to give but not always easy to take. The solutions that worked for typical parents may not be right for you and your toddler. In a blog post titled "Being an Autistic Parent" shared by Asperger/Autistic Network (AANE), Aria Sky, agender late-diagnosed Autistic parent of autistic children, wrote: "Mainstream parenting advice and expectations didn't work for me at all, but I had no idea at the time why, which was frustrating (to say the least). So I focused on finding workable alternatives. Looking back, I believe it was mostly sensory issues that led me to my unconventional parenting practices."

Like Aria Sky, you can trust your own parenting instincts when bombarded with well-intended but unsolicited advice. If someone tells you that you should spank your child for having a tantrum or that you shouldn't use a leash-like safety harness in a crowded place, you don't have to respond. If it's a stranger, it's fine to ignore them or give a simple, brief, or one-word acknowledgment such as "Thanks" or "That's an idea." (You didn't say it was a good idea, did you?) Then move away from them if you can and continue to do what's right for you and your toddler.

Unwanted advice can be anything from "You shouldn't breastfeed your child at this age" to "You should still be breast-feeding your child," or from "You should let your child cry it out" to "You should pick your child up immediately each time they cry." The suggestions can directly contradict each other, and each person who gives advice believes that their idea is correct.

But if it's not right for you and your family, don't do it.

If someone close to you, such as a family member or a good friend, gives you advice, bear in mind that they care for you and they're trying to be helpful. Prepare a stock reply or script such as "Thank you for the idea, but we've discussed this issue (or we've talked to our pediatrician) and we've decided …" or "Thank you for the idea. I'll talk about it with my partner (or pediatrician)."

TODDLER COMMUNICATION

One of the hardest things about being a toddler is that they're old enough to know exactly what they want, but their communication skills haven't developed enough for them to let you know. If they want an orange but they don't know the word for it, they might say "nana," because a banana may seem similar to them. They will refuse the banana that is offered and then try "ball." When they are

3: Toddlers & Preschoolers

given a toy ball, they may even say "nana ball" in a final attempt to communicate that they want an orange. If their parents still don't understand, the situation may end with a meltdown.

Toddlers need visual supports on their path to better communication. If the toddler in the situation above had a picture of an orange they could point to, it would have saved some time and tears. Consider taking photographs of the usual items your toddler asks for and putting them into a binder or small photo wallet. Include pictures of things you have available and are willing for them to have; for example, don't have a picture of a candy bar if they can't have one, but do include pictures of the various kinds of food items and toys that they often ask for and may have.

There's no need to worry that they won't learn to speak using words if they have access to using pictures. As their language skills develop, it will be much easier for them to say, "I want an orange," than it is for them to get out the book, find the page, and point to the picture of the orange. During the months when they cannot yet say what they want and be understood, it will help them learn the power of communication and fend off frustration and meltdowns.

The act of completed communication is powerful. If they are unable to let you know that they want the cereal shaped like little balls, not like O-shaped circles with a hole in the middle, it can be terribly frustrating. If only they could find the word, you could give them the right cereal. Sometimes just knowing that you get it helps. When you say you understand which kind of cereal they want, but that kind is all gone so how about the O-shaped cereal instead, it might help them accept the less-preferred option. At least they communicated, and communication is a powerful tool.

SIBLING STRESS

In many families, the toddler and preschool years is the time when another child is welcomed into the family. Unfortunately, it's not always a joyful occasion for your little first-born. Reducing the stress of a new sibling will take mindfulness and advance planning, but it is possible. Some tips to remember: SIS & BRO: Schedule time, Increase privileges & responsibility, Separate spaces, & Bond with baby, Reverse the story, Only-child date.

SIS & BRO

Schedule Time
The S in SIS & BRO is for Scheduling Time.

If you have good intentions to spend more time with your first child, but you don't put it on the calendar, chances are it won't happen. You know you want to spend extra time with your child before and after the new baby comes home, but to make it a reality, schedule that time on the calendar, in ink. Making it definite will ensure that your child knows that they are still a priority in your life, even though there's a new baby now.

3: Toddlers & Preschoolers

Increase Privileges & Responsibility
The I in SIS & BRO is for Increasing Privileges
and Responsibility.

Becoming a big brother or big sister is a good time to increase both privileges and responsibilities. New privileges might include being able to choose the music to play at the baby's bedtime, or getting a bigger bed or chair. New responsibilities might be bringing the diaper bag to Dad or Mom when it's time for a diaper change for the new baby, or finding a toy or rattle to cheer the baby up.

Separate Spaces
The second S in SIS & BRO is for Separate Spaces.

Even if they love the new baby, it's important for your firstborn to have separate spaces whenever possible. If they must share a bedroom, you might declare that during their afternoon nap time, their room is a no-babies-allowed zone. Having time apart will help them appreciate their time together.

Bond with Baby
The B in SIS & BRO is for Bonding with Baby.

Create special activities for your kids to bond with each other. It might be when the older sibling sings a special song during diaper changes or does a silly dance to cheer up the baby when they're crying.

Parenting While Autistic

Reverse the Story

The R in SIS & BRO is for Reversing the Story.

It's inevitable that your older child will often hear you say, "Later; I have to feed the baby first," or "Not right now; the baby needs a clean diaper." For a change, reverse the story. When you do something for your older child, tell the baby, "Wait, baby, I'm getting some juice for your big brother now," or "I'll hold you pretty soon, baby, right now I'm reading a story to your big sister." Hearing that they're not the only ones who are told "Wait" will help them gain perspective on what it means to have a new baby in the family. Sure, the baby will need a lot of care and attention, but not all of it. Big brothers and sisters are also important and valued, and occasionally the baby has to wait their turn for attention, too.

Only Child Date

The O in SIS & BRO is for Only-Child Dates.

As often as you can manage it, arrange for each of your children to have Only Child Dates with each parent. You can call it "Mommy-Joey" time or "Daddy-Ayesha" time. Whatever you call it, put it on the calendar and make sure you give each child their own date with each parent. It could be as simple as a trip to the grocery store with just the two of you, or a trip to the park, or whatever would be special for them. This is their opportunity to imagine they're an only child. If they're old enough to understand calendars and recognize their written name, it will mean a lot to see it on the calendar. If they're too young for calendars, consider giving them an anticipation schedule. Three to five days before the event, put colorful sticky notes on the fridge, one for each day until they go on their special date. Every day count them together, take one down, then count how many are left. When you get to the last sticky note, that means it's time to go on the Only-Child Date. Just be sure to place them high enough that your child can't take them off themselves.

SENSORY SMARTS

Toddlers are sensory magnets and magnifiers. They find things to touch, smell, and taste everywhere they go. They also provide a high level of sensory input for anyone nearby, whether they're squealing in delight, screeching in protest, bringing you a flower they picked, or filling up their diaper. Their greatest need for a cuddle may come at a time when you feel all "touched out" and cannot bear any more skin contact. If you spend a day with a toddler, expect to be exhausted by sensory stimulation.

How can you cope with the onslaught? By being prepared.

Try ear protection that allows you to hear what's going on while softening the aural impact of blocks being knocked down or of tiny feet tromping down the hall and into your skull. For safety's sake you need to be able to hear them, but not at full volume. Research the various options, including loop types, ear plugs, and noise-reducing headphones.

Parenting While Autistic

Pretending to eat the mud pies a child makes for a pretend tea party is a time-honored bit of acting that parents have excelled at for generations. Even if your young chef made their pie out of foods mixed together rather than mud, or even if they're trying to cram a bite of their lunch into your mouth to share the experience, you're not obligated to eat it. Practice the sleight-of-hand to disappear the unwanted food morsel before it gets inserted between your lips and pretend you have gobbled it down.

A dab of scented lotion or oil under your nose can help fend off the many and various smells that your little angel is capable of creating, especially during toilet training. If your preschooler is into fingerpainting but the smell of the tempera mixture gives you a headache, consider letting them fingerpaint with pudding on a large, smooth, unbreakable plate or choosing one of the edible fingerpaint recipes available on the internet.

Just because you have sensory issues doesn't mean you can't enjoy the world with your sensory-seeking toddler or preschooler.

MAKE FAMILY MEETINGS FUN

When your little one is old enough to sit at a table or attend preschool story time, consider inviting them to a Family Meeting. The only item on the agenda might be, "What shall we have for dessert tonight, cookies or ice cream?" Your preschooler votes, it's approved, and that night, when they see their chosen dessert on the table, they see for themselves the value of participating in Family

Meetings. Of course, you should only offer two choices for young children, and make sure both choices are available and parent-approved before offering.

You'll still need to have your own Family Meetings for parents to synchronize your calendars, but don't expect your little one to sit through the business part of the meeting. Their first experience of Family Meetings should be 100% positive to set the stage for their continuing participation as they grow.

WEEKENDS THAT WORK

For those who work predictable hours during the week and have weekends off, those precious two days may have been your opportunity to sleep in as late as you want and take your time to check the news, read, catch up on social media, binge-watch your favorite shows, and enjoy your leisure.

Now that you have a toddler, those days seem long gone. Once they wake up, the world revolves around them. It's age-appropriate for them to assume that you'd much rather play with them than do anything else, and it shows a healthy security in your love for them. You want to provide that 24/7 unconditional love, but you also want some time to yourself. How do you manage it?

Tag Team Parenting

Tag Team Parenting is when you take turns with being there for your little one and having time for yourself. In some families, it may mean that on Saturdays one parent gets up when your toddler wakes up and the other one is guaranteed a couple of extra hours of sleep or privacy. On Sundays, they reverse the roles.

Another way to manage weekends is that on alternating Saturdays the parents take turns being the one "on duty," and Sundays are for the whole family. This might be your family time to make a big breakfast together, go to worship, take a picnic to a park, visit grandparents or friends, or do whatever your family loves to do. Here are some weekend tips:

- Know in advance where you're going and what to expect.
- Plan for transitions between weekend activities using pictures or visual schedules.
- Bring snacks so your little one doesn't get hungry and cranky.
- Have toys, board books, teethers, and busy blankets attached to the car seat or stroller so they won't be lost if they are dropped.
- Don't skip their naptime if they're used to napping each day.
- Plan for recovery time after social events.

With a little planning you can create a weekend that works for all of you.

FICTIONAL FAMILIES

Trish & Bill, Autistic Parents

Jim-Jim, as baby James was affectionately called, was the joy of Trish and Bill's world. As he learned to walk and talk, he provided constant entertainment for them. He was also the source of exhaustion and sensory overload, although his parents would never think to fault him for it. He was a toddler, after all, so it was his job to be curious about the world around him. Their job was to keep him alive in spite of his adventurous inclinations, and to make sure he knew he was loved and cared for.

For the first year of his life, Trish had taken extended parenting leave from her job at the university. Bill worked from home, but just because he was there all day didn't mean he could drop his work to take care of Jim-Jim, so she felt staying home was what they needed. They had been able to make ends meet with just Bill's salary, since their needs were simple, but after Jim-Jim's first birthday, the university started emailing Trish to ask when she would return to work.

Even thinking about leaving her baby five days a week made her stomach hurt. At the same time, she felt some loyalty to the university she had attended as a student. They had given Trish her first and only job, and she had met Bill at a university lecture.

After ignoring their emails and worrying for a few weeks, she brought it up at their next Family Meeting after Jim-Jim was down for the night.

Parenting While Autistic

"I just don't know how I can leave you both and go back to the office," she said.

"Are you sure you have to? We could go on as we are now." Bill loved it when things went on the same way they had started; change was not easy for him.

"The thing is, we could use the extra money. And I really enjoyed the work I did for the university."

"If you love it, you should go back." Bill's heart fell, but he knew he needed to let Trish do what made her happy.

"I love you and Jim-Jim more. And even though I loved the work, I did not love having to be around people all day. It was exhausting!"

"Yeah, I get that. That's why I work from home. I just couldn't take the whole office politics nonsense." Bill felt a brightness, as if an actual light bulb had lit up over his head, flooding him with a brilliant idea. "I know! You should work from home, like I do."

"Do you think they'd let me?"

"Of course! They must know how valuable you are to them or they wouldn't be emailing you to come back. Anyway, if you don't at least ask for what you want, you'll never know if they might have said yes."

"You're right, of course." Trish bit her lip. "It's just so hard for me to ask for things."

"What's the worst that could happen? Will they hit you over the head with a pool noodle?" Bill loved to make Trish giggle. "Will they yell at you and call you a silly ninnyhammer?"

3: Toddlers & Preschoolers

"Of course not!" Trish couldn't keep from laughing. "But they might say no."

"True. But they might say yes."

She knew he was right. After writing and rewriting an email asking to work from home and running it past Bill for his input, she finally hit send.

What a relief it was to learn that the university was happy to arrange a flexible, work-from-home plan for her. She decided she didn't want to work full time-yet, but there were several projects she enjoyed that she could do remotely.

At their next Family Meeting, Trish and Bill made up a schedule and put it on a big calendar on the wall. They needed to see exactly when each of them would be working and undisturbed, when they would be minding Jim-Jim full time so the other could work, and when they would both be off the clock together. The schedule allowed them time to focus on work, family time, alone time to decompress, and time for the two of them to spend together.

Over the weeks and months of toddlerhood and preschool, their plan changed as needed. They brought up problems in their Family Meetings so they could address them and make necessary changes before little problems became big resentments. They had found the perfect solution for their little family.

Parenting While Autistic

Justin & Maggie, Autistic Dad Adoption Story

"What's wrong with him?" Maggie hugged her own arms as tightly as Justin hugged their screaming son.

"There's nothing wrong with him." He dodged a tiny fist, wrapped the boy's arms more snugly in his own, and got kicked a few times before managing to get them both into the rocking chair.

"I know there's nothing wrong with *him*, but why is he screaming?" She sometimes got exasperated when Justin took her words literally, but at the same time she wanted to train herself not to use that kind of vague questioning with their precious child. They were a neurodiversity-affirming family, and there was nothing wrong with that. But what was causing all the screaming? The meltdowns were happening more and more frequently, sometimes several times a day, and the bigger he grew, the harder he was to contain and keep safe when he lost control.

At last, he seemed to be winding down, and Justin sang softly in his ear as he cuddled and rocked him.

"It's okay, Ray. It's okay, Ray. Ray-Ray, Ray-Ray, it's okay." He always sang it the same way each time, softly and in a gentle monotone. It was working—Ray drifted off to sleep in his father's arms.

Ray had come to them with the birth name Rainbow Majesty, and they didn't want to keep that name or confuse him with something completely different, so they called him Ray. In time they would legally change it to Raymond M. something. Raymond Malcolm? Raymond Mark? Or maybe they'd leave Majesty as

3: Toddlers & Preschoolers

his middle name. There was plenty of time to decide before the adoption would be final and they would need to document his new name on the paperwork.

At the moment, little Ray was sleeping peacefully, looking like an angel.

"So, what do you think it was about this time?" Maggie whispered. "Was it because I spilled the beans?" She had quite literally spilled half a bag of dried black beans on the kitchen floor, and before she could turn around, there was Ray, giggling while he moved the hard beans around on the floor with his hands and picked them up to drop them and hear the sound they made. Because the beans were so small, Maggie knew they were a choking hazard, so she swooped in to pick him up and put him in his play space with a baby gate between him and the kitchen. His wails as she cleaned up the beans were pitiful, and they kept escalating. By the time the last bean was off the floor and she went to get him, he was in a full meltdown and didn't even seem to hear anything she said.

Fortunately, Justin was there and was able to get him to sleep, finally.

"I'm not sure. Maybe. He sure seemed to love those beans. Can't he play with them? It would feel great to be able to put your hands into a big bin of beans and just sift them in your fingers."

"It might feel great, but you know he'd put them in his mouth."

"Yeah, he would. So, what can we give him that would feel like that, and sound cool when dropped on the floor, that he couldn't choke on?"

Parenting While Autistic

"I don't know." Maggie hadn't thought about trying to replicate the aspects of the experience that he loved in a safer format. "What kind of big things can you sift, and when you drop them, they make a sound, but they're too big to choke on?"

After they transferred Ray to his crib to finish his nap, they did some research online. They needed toys that would provide the same sensory experience, without the choking hazard. Two things seemed like they might fit the bill.

One was a toddler-safe set of building bricks. Justin had always loved them, but the regular bricks were tiny and unsafe. The large size was just right for little hands and too big to choke on. He didn't yet have the dexterity to put them together properly, but if he had a bin of them, he could play with them with his hands and listen to the sounds they made when he dropped them on the floor. They ordered a set and a plastic shoe box to store them in.

The other idea was a set of plastic rings. These could be strung together to attach a toy to a stroller or car seat, hold plastic teething keys, or be purchased separately in sets of eight. They seemed like they would make the right kind of sound if dropped, so they ordered two sets and a small storage bin.

After the items arrived, the couple tried first one and then the other to see if Ray had a strong preference. He seemed to love them both and spent long periods of time with them, running his hands through the bins, tossing them, and giggling when they landed with a clatter on the floor. These became the family's go-to sensory bins when he seemed bored and started to get into mischief by seeing how high he could climb on the furniture. Once the bins appeared, he was happy to come down from the refrigerator and play on the floor.

Other things that helped with his tantrums included paying attention to his naptime and feeding schedules. Being hungry or sleepy could easily trigger a meltdown. Knowing what Ray needed as far as food, sleep, and sensory stimulation helped Justin and Maggie do their best to maintain a happy, balanced household during the "Dramatic Twos" and the "Thrill-Seeking Threes."

Lucia & Naima, Two Autistic Moms

"Did you read the paperwork I gave you about the preschools?" Naima had been researching local preschools and wanted Lucia's opinions.

"Not yet." Lucia stood, picked up the plates from the table, and carried them to the kitchen. Naima followed her.

"Why not? You know we have to decide if we want a good one."

"Isn't it too soon, though? Ruby's just a baby." They had shortened Precious Ruby to simply Ruby. It was easy to say and she responded to it, and Lucia knew it held a special place in Naima's heart, since she had lost her Grandma Ruby.

"She's not a baby; she's a toddler, almost a preschooler, about to become a proud, independent woman. What she needs is the right start in the right school." Naima started loading the dishwasher.

They both froze for a moment at a sound from the baby monitor, then sighed in unison when they heard a tiny, adorable snore.

Parenting While Autistic

"I'm just not ready to let her go spend her days with strangers." Lucia wiped down the kitchen counter, circling the same spot with her sponge again and again.

"I think that spot's clean now," Naima said gently. "And I think you're worried. Let's talk."

They brought the baby monitor and glasses of wine and sat down in the living room. Lucia realized she had been worrying about this and avoiding reading about the preschool options that Naima kept pushing at her. Finally, she spoke.

"You're right: I am worried. I don't want to put Ruby in preschool yet. I just don't think she's ready."

"You don't think she's ready, or you don't think you're ready?" Naima took her hand. "What are you afraid of?"

"How long do you have?" She chuckled but didn't sound happy.

"I have all the time in the world. Talk to me."

"Okay, here goes. I'm worried that the teachers won't care about her like we do. I'm worried that the other kids won't like her or will bully her. I'm worried that she'll fall off something and get hurt. I'm worried that the teachers will be mean to her. I'm worried that she will feel sad and alone, and she'll cry for us, and we won't be there. I don't want to let her down or put her in harm's way." Lucia sighed. "Can't we just teach her at home? What does she need to learn in preschool anyway? Colors? Numbers? Shapes?"

"How about how to play with other kids her age? We can't teach her that at home. She needs to be around other kids."

3: Toddlers & Preschoolers

"But what if she doesn't know how to play like they do? What if she's excluded, left out, all alone in a crowd? And what if she's the only kid there with two mommies and no daddy? What will they think?"

"They'll think how lucky she is to have two such amazing moms, that's what."

"I'm serious."

"So am I." Naima put down her glass. "Look, when I was a kid, I never knew how to play with the other kids. They all seemed to know how to play together, how to make friends, and it was a mystery to me."

"Yeah," Lucia sighed. "Me, too. That's why I don't want to put her in school."

"That's why we need to put her in school. Look, you and I, we're autistic. We struggled in school because we couldn't just learn all that social stuff automatically like the other kids; we had to teach ourselves how to observe and imitate."

"Sometimes it was horrible."

"Same. I know. But Ruby's not like us. She's not autistic."

"How do you know that?"

"You've seen her with her cousins or at the church nursery. When she sees other little kids, she is totally into them. She never hesitates or has to watch them and figure out how to play, she just plays. Social stuff is natural for her."

Lucia smiled. "Yeah, it is. Our daughter's a social genius."

Parenting While Autistic

"I won't argue about the genius part, because we both know that's right. But her social superpowers are typical, just like all the other little kids she'll meet in preschool. And she's going to love it."

It took a few more heart-to-heart talks, but eventually Lucia read the preschool information, they visited a few on their own, and they took Ruby to see the one they liked best. As soon as they got in the door, she took off running to join the kids and was laughing and playing almost immediately. She looked so happy, so comfortable with a group of kids. Lucia didn't understand the feeling personally, but she couldn't deny that Ruby loved it. Soon they signed the paperwork and Ruby was an official student. They started in the two-day-a-week program, and as Ruby grew, she graduated into the three-day program, and eventually she went to school five mornings a week. She thrived and blossomed at school. Lucia and Naima knew that they had made the right decision for their daughter, even though it had not been an easy one. Sometimes the most difficult decisions lead to the greatest outcomes.

Maria & Santiago, Undiagnosed Autistic Mom

What started as a three-month visit for Graciela turned into two years, as she worried that her daughter would not be able to handle caring for twins alone. Santiago seemed like another burden rather than a helpmate for Maria. But soon after the twins' second birthday, her own husband had a minor heart attack, so she moved back home to care for him. When he had retired and been underfoot constantly, she had been happy to stay with Maria and only see him

3: Toddlers & Preschoolers

a few times a week, but now he needed her. She knew her duty, and now it was with her husband. Maria and Santiago would have to learn how to manage their lives without her.

Santiago was exultant when his mother-in-law moved out. He had felt more and more pushed aside in a female house with no place for him. Now, he was the father and breadwinner, the king of his own domain. Unfortunately, there was trouble in the castle.

Maria was a loving mother who doted on her daughters, but sometimes she just, well, broke. He couldn't think of another way to describe it. One minute she'd be sweetly singing to them, fixing them little sandwiches with the crusts cut off just so, and all was well with the world. Then suddenly, she would break. She'd be sitting on the floor, hands over her ears, crying uncontrollably. She didn't even stop crying when he yelled at her to stop. What else was he supposed to do?

It took a lot of trial and error for Maria and Santiago to learn how to work together to care for their little ones, and it is to their credit that they did. While he didn't understand why, Santiago knew that his girls needed their naps or they'd transform instantly from sweet to salty, ready for a fight over anything or nothing. So he helped remind Maria to put them down for naps every day. The upside of that was, when Maria spent their nap time alone in her room, she didn't fall apart like she used to. No matter how much she adored them, she needed time away from the girls every day.

It wasn't always easy to put two active little girls to bed at night. They were so interested in everything that they didn't want to settle down to sleep. When Faith finally drifted off, Hope would tickle her and wake her up. When Hope fell asleep, Faith would hit her with her stuffed rabbit. Maria and Santiago were at their wits' end, and their own sleep deprivation was taking its toll.

One day, when Maria looked like she was about to break again, Santiago bundled up the twins into their car seats and started driving. He told Maria to get some rest for herself and that he wouldn't come home until both girls were asleep. Faith and Hope were thrilled with this idea. They loved looking out the windows at the trees and buildings going by. Santiago started singing "The Wheels on the Bus," always a hit, but after a couple of times through, he was done. He switched the radio on to sports. That was enough to bore the girls to sleep. When he got home, he transferred them from car seats to double stroller, and then inside and into their beds without waking them. For the first time, Santiago felt like a good father. He still didn't understand his wife, but he had found something he could do for his family that made a difference. It felt great.

Robert & Helen, Grandparenting While Autistic

"Helen, I've got a problem, and I don't know what to do." Robert drummed his fingers rhythmically on the kitchen table, looking away from her out the window.

"What is it?" Helen poured him a cup of coffee and sat down beside him. "Let's figure it out together."

3: Toddlers & Preschoolers

"I don't know how to play with Bobby." Robert couldn't look at her. He felt ashamed, but he trusted his wife.

"I'm not sure what you mean. You just—play."

"Well, I never played when I was a kid, I just rode my bike and collected junk. And I never played with Lena when she was little. I worked, and you took care of her, and that was that." He sighed. "But now I'm a grandpa, and I don't know the rules."

"There are no rules for playing with a three-year-old."

"There are, and he knows them. He starts banging around with his action figures, and I try to join in, but apparently, I do it wrong. I try to make my action guy say something or do something, and he says, 'No, Gwampa,' and takes it away and does his own thing with it."

"I'm sure if you just keep trying, you two will figure something out. The important thing is to play with him, not how you play."

"Well, there's another thing." His fingers started drumming a little faster.

"Okay, spit it out. What's eating at you?"

"I just—well, I just …" Robert shook his hands out and cracked his knuckles. Helen winced, but she didn't interrupt him to ask him not to do that. She could see that he was upset, and she knew from experience that if she tried to push him or break his train of thought, she might never find out what he was trying to say. After a pause he began again.

"The truth is, Helen, I just don't like playing." He went on before she could say anything. "I know, it's terrible, probably a character

Parenting While Autistic

flaw. You know how much I love Bobby. I'd do anything for that boy, but I don't like playing. I feel awkward and tongue-tied, like I'm failing at being a grandfather."

Helen put her hand over his. "You are a wonderful grandfather, Robert. No one could love that boy more than you do."

"Then why can't I play, like a normal grandpa?"

"I don't know; maybe it's just not your style." Helen thought for a moment. "Maybe you could find something else to do with him, something special between the two of you, that doesn't involve playing with action figures?"

"Like what?"

"I don't know." Helen thought. Bobby was too young to put together models or construction bricks, or to help Robert tinker with broken television sets and parts. They sat quietly for a few moments, each of them thinking of ideas and discarding them as not worth mentioning. Finally, Robert broke the silence.

"I've got it! A Thing-Finding Walk!"

Helen smiled. "What is a Thing-Finding Walk? Or do I even need to ask?"

"Exactly what it says it is. We go for a walk. We find things."

"You're not going to take him to the junk yard to help you look for old TV parts, are you?"

"Of course not! I know he's too young for that. That'll have to wait until he's four." He smiled his lopsided smile so Helen knew he was joking.

"All right, then. What will you find?"

3: Toddlers & Preschoolers

"Things. You know, rocks, feathers, leaves. We'll know it when we see it."

"So this will be your regular Bobby-Grandpa time together?"

"Yep. Every afternoon, right after, his nap, we'll go for a walk together."

"That's a lovely idea, Robert. I'm sure Bobby will love it."

And he did. The two of them looked forward to their walks, and they always found fascinating things to see, talk about, and bring home. Robert didn't know that he was autistic back in those days, but he knew he needed a different way to connect with his grandson that worked for both of them.

Daisy & Crow, Fur-Baby Parents

(Crow and Daisy take a pizza out of the oven as Kitty comes in with Bugbear on a leash.)

KITTY: Hi, honeys, we're home!

DAISY: Thanks for walking him. He loves his walkies, don't you, my little bugsy-wugsy?

CROW: Did he do his business? And did you clean up after him?

KITTY: Yes, and yes.

DAISY: You're just in time for pizza. Can you stay again?

KITTY: Yeah, thanks, I'd love to.

CROW: Do you need to call your parents, so they won't worry about you?

KITTY: They won't worry.

CROW: Kitty, you're fourteen. It seems like they ought to be worrying. Should I call them?

Parenting While Autistic

KITTY: No way. Kids my age have sleepovers all the time. They won't even notice I'm gone.

CROW: That sounds wrong.

DAISY: So how are your parents adjusting to having a daughter?

KITTY: They—I—It's a hard thing to wrap their minds around. They're better off if I stay out of the house for a while.

CROW: You're sure? You've been here all weekend. Don't want them to think we kidnapped you.

KITTY: I'm sure. In fact, uh, they said I could stay longer if I want. If it's okay with you guys.

CROW: They said that? You talked to them?

DAISY: Of course, you can stay as long as you want! Bugbear loves his Kitty, don't you, Bug-Bug?

CROW: What about school?

KITTY: I can catch the bus at the corner. And I've got my backpack and clothes and stuff. But I don't want to get in the way here if you want me to go.

CROW: You're not in the way; we love having you. I just don't want the police knocking on our door looking for you because your parents reported you missing or anything.

KITTY: My parents will not report me missing, you can count on that. So, I can stay?

DAISY: Of course, you can! Mi couch es su couch!

CROW: That's not how—

DAISY: *(puts a slice of pizza into Crow's open mouth, mid-sentence)* Like I said, our couch is your couch. For as long as you need it.

3: Toddlers & Preschoolers

PARENT TO PARENT

"My wife and I decided that it would be me that would stay home with the kids and raise them. That was a mutual agreement, as we tried different arrangements for raising our kids. Me staying home seem to work the best for the both of us. After my child became one, I bought a Dr. Brazelton book called *TouchPoints: Birth to Three* (1992, 2009, 2021, Hachette Books). I read that book religiously and followed the instructions given.

"One thing I noticed early on was that it was almost impossible for me to do the things I enjoyed, because the kids needed my attention, and switching from my entertainment to their needs proved to be too emotionally challenging for me. I decided that I would do the things they were interested in. I got very good at video games, to the point where they would call me to help them through a certain game level. That's not the case with electronic gadgets these days, by any means. I would also have tea parties with my daughter. She liked to look for bugs with me, too, until the day her mom ran screaming about a moth in the house. That put an end to our bug exploration days."

— James, late-diagnosed autistic dad

"The 24/7 nature of toddlers meant that I got very little time for my stim behavior (embroidery and knitting) and that left me feeling really depleted. I remember when my youngest was four years old and had a reliable bedtime routine, I felt like I got my life back, because I could once again embroider in the evenings.

Parenting While Autistic

I would encourage autistic parents to plan ahead for this. Find family members that can give you a weekly 'recovery' day, or trade childcare with friends so you each get a day off, or plan your finances so that you can afford childcare when you need recovery time. The toddler years are fun and wondrous but also quite demanding, so you want to think about what you need to pace yourself through this stage of parenting."

— Krista, autistic mom

Chapter 4

Elementary School

The Kids Are All Right

"One of the most important gifts a parent can give a child is the gift of accepting that child's uniqueness."

— Fred Rogers

"There are only two lasting bequests we can hope to give our children. One of these is roots, the other, wings."

— Johann Wolfgang von Goethe

4: Elementary School

CHANGES

As your child grows, there will be many changes. Most autistic parents are not fond of change; life is so much more comfortable and safer when it follows the same routines. However, when it comes to parenthood, expect the unexpected. It can be difficult to prepare for all the changes in store for you. Difficult, but not impossible. By creating systems and organization tools, you can take the unexpected in stride.

The key is PLAN B: Prepare, Learn, Accommodate, Negotiate, and Build slowly.

PLAN B

Prepare
The P in PLAN B is for Prepare.

Prepare for the unexpected whenever possible. Seems like a contradiction in terms, but use what you know to prepare for what you don't yet know. If you know that your child's class will be going on a field trip or having a book fair, science fair, Open House, or school concert, find out all you can about it. Chances are your child's school has a website. Check out their yearly calendar and transfer important dates to your own calendar, with prompts to alert you at least two weeks in advance. Think about what will be needed. Some will be expected, such as a backpack, binder, pencils, and other school supplies. The website, or a group email from your child's teacher, will let you know what to shop for. Then look ahead at the bigger events throughout the year to see what else they might need. A sleeping bag for the Outdoor School Camp experience? Black pants and a white shirt to perform in the school concert? A cardboard trifold for a science project display? Whatever needs are likely to come up during the year, knowing what to expect will help you prepare for the many events that are part of being the parent of a school kid.

Learn
The L in PLAN B is for Learn.

Learn all you can about your child's school, academic expectations, and school rules. Your online preparation will give you a lot of this information. You can find out about parent-teacher meetings and what the school expects from parents. Do they want parents to attend every large group meeting or just the one-on-one parent teacher conferences? Do they need classroom supplies, or snacks, or cupcakes for a bake sale? Learn the rules before you donate baked goods; many schools only accept store-bought, individually packaged treats, and not every classroom celebrates birthdays or holidays at school. If you'll be driving your child to school, take a practice run ahead of the first day to see where the drop off/pick up lanes are. Expect it to be crowded on school days, so leave the house early enough that you won't be stressing while stuck in the parking lot traffic jam. If they'll take a bus, learn about the bus routes and rules, and how snow days or late pick-up days will be communicated. Will someone email you, or are you expected to log in on the website to find out about changes in schedules? The more you learn, the more relaxed you can feel about this next step in your child's education.

Accommodate

The A in PLAN B is for Accommodate.

You can accommodate your child by making sure they have what they need to do their best work in school. This includes making sure they are well-rested and have a healthy breakfast and lunch. If your child is also neurodivergent or has another identified learning difficulty, they may have an Individualized Education Program (IEP) or a 504 plan under the Americans with Disabilities Act (ADA). Their plan will include accommodations they might need in the classroom.

But what about parent accommodations?

If you choose to disclose your neurodivergence to your child's school, they may be more understanding if you ask for accommodations when attending school meetings. Do you need to stand at the back so you can step outside if there are too many people and sensory distractions? Do you want all communications to be in writing as well as verbal so that you can review the parent-teacher meeting notes later when you're not under stress? Do you need to wear headphones or dark glasses in meetings to protect yourself from auditory and visual overload? You may not need to tell the school anything and may just quietly take care of accommodating your own needs without drawing attention to yourself. However, if you want them to know about your neurodivergence and to realize that you're not being rude, you may choose to share with them that you are an autistic parent. To tell or not to tell is a personal decision which is yours alone to make.

Negotiate
The N in PLAN B is for Negotiate.

If your child is in the neuro-majority, they may enjoy things that would be difficult for you. Perhaps they want to go to a crowded pizza place with a ball pit, arcade games, singing animatronic characters, and a guy in an animal mascot costume, while dozens of kids race around and shriek in delight. Is this your child's dream but your nightmare? Then it's time to negotiate. You won't be able to tolerate this as a weekly or even monthly treat if you are highly sensitive to loud or unexpected sounds, flashing lights, and competing smells. Can you tolerate it annually? If so, it can be a birthday present. If you can't manage that, then consider hosting your child's actual birthday party with cake and presents quietly at home or at a restful park. At another time, see if you can arrange for a family member who likes that kind of excitement to take them to the pizza restaurant. They can enjoy all the sensory-rich activities without you having to be there yourself if it would be an impossibility for you.

4: Elementary School

Most things can be negotiated. The important thing is to let your child know that their wants and needs are heard and respected and that you will try to find a way to meet the appropriate ones. At the same time, they should respect that you have different needs. Thinking about others' needs as well as their own is part of the transition from being a preschool little kid to becoming an elementary school big kid.

Build Slowly
The B in PLAN B is for Build slowly.

It's important to build slowly as you meet the various stages and changes in your child's growth. Each child learns and grows differently, and there is no rush to a finish line. Most children learn to read naturally between the ages of four and eight years. If your child isn't reading fluently at age six, that doesn't mean there's a problem. Schools are geared for children to meet certain academic milestones at specific times, but that's not necessarily the way your child, or any child, will develop naturally. There's nothing wrong with that, and you shouldn't worry. If you look at a class of four-year-olds and one of them is already reading, that child might appear remarkable. If you look at the class when they're six years old and one of them isn't reading at all yet, you might imagine they're not as smart as the rest. But if you wait and look at the group when they're ten years old and all of them are reading, you probably can't tell which ones started reading early and which ones started later. Everybody's reading now, and that's the way it's supposed to be. Allow your child to build as slowly as they need to, and let them achieve their next learning steps in their own good time.

SOCIAL SCHEDULES

Most kids are social beings. They love to play together with other kids their age. The problem is, they can't drive yet; they're just kids. After school, they rely on you to help them make the social connections they crave. If you grew up autistic, it might not seem important to you, but ask your child how they feel. Do they want to hang out with other kids after school, on weekends, and during vacations? Or are they perfectly happy to spend school breaks as family time and see their classmates again when they get back to school? Their preference may change as they progress from kindergarten toward middle school, so be prepared to keep up with their changing needs.

If you have a little social butterfly, but you'd rather stay cozy in the comfort of your home, you may need to find creative ways to help them meet their social needs. A play date with one classmate may be just the thing. This may include a trip to the park, so let's use PARK to remember some key points: Parents, Anticipate, Reciprocate, and Keep it simple.

4: Elementary School

PARK

Parents
The P in PARK is for Parents.

First, try to get to know the other parents in your child's class, especially parents of the kids your child talks about the most. You might meet them at a parent meeting or when you drop off and pick up your kids. Introduce yourself, not only with your own name, but also with your identity as "Claire's dad" or "Jack's mom." Then make sure you say "Hi" to them each time you see them. When you're more comfortable being around them, you might ask if they want to get the kids together at a nearby park after school.

Second, think about your own parents and in-laws. Many grandparents would love to take their grandchild to a park, fast food playground, or children's museum and watch them socialize informally with other kids. Your parents might even step up to take your child to a birthday party or structured play date if you don't feel up to the social demands. Grandparents can be lifesavers. Trust them to have your back when you need them!

Anticipate
The A in PARK is for Anticipate.

Anticipate what will be the most difficult part of a play date for you. Is it socializing with the other parent? Then consider an activity such as miniature golf or visiting a petting zoo or pumpkin patch, rather than just sitting on a park bench next to a virtual stranger. Do you hate to be outside in the bright sun? Find an indoor art class for kids. It doesn't matter which part of a play date is the hardest one for you to cope with; knowing in advance what to expect, what will be difficult, and what strategies you can put into place will help make it manageable.

Reciprocate
The R in PARK is for Reciprocate.

If another parent is always inviting your child over to play with their child, it's going to seem one-sided if you don't reciprocate. Take turns thinking of something to do with the kids, and ask them sometimes, rather than always waiting to be asked. If you never invite them to do something or suggest a shared activity, they may assume you don't like them or that your child doesn't like their child. If you're not comfortable having people in your home, go to a playground, park, or children's museum. The important thing to model for your child is the importance of taking turns.

Keep It Simple
The K in PARK is for Keep It Simple.

This is the most important thing to remember. Keep it simple. You don't have to orchestrate a play date extravaganza to end all extravaganzas. Kids don't care about the hoopla; they just want to play. Providing them with a place to play is a great start. If you're at a park or playground, the swings and slides are already there. If they come over to your house on a rainy day, paper and crayons or a board game might be all you need. Even a birthday party doesn't need to be extreme as long as the kids have something to do, like a simple art activity or game. It's not necessary to hire a magician, pony ride, clown, or princess to make an appearance; just let the kids be kids. They'll have fun.

SCHOOL COMMUNICATION

No matter what grade your kids are in, it's important to stay in communication with their teachers. Offering to volunteer will go a long way toward helping an overworked teacher feel supported.

Do they need a room parent? If you have the time but you're not comfortable volunteering in the classroom, that's okay. Just because you don't want to be in the room with all of the kids and the noise and the smells and fluorescent lights doesn't mean you can't help. Ask your child's teacher what kind of craft or office support they need. Most teachers are thrilled to have a helper who will cut out paper shapes for bulletin board displays, or make copies, or staple together homework packets. They will be grateful to have your help with any of the tasks that you can do from the office or from home.

If your child has special needs, they may have an IEP. This is a formal plan that documents your child's strengths and needs, goals, and progress toward achieving those goals. It's important to attend IEP meetings when they're called. If they schedule one for a time that you can't be there, you have a right to ask for a different time. If they put anything in the IEP that you don't understand, ask. If you disagree with what they wrote, tell them, and help them get it right. This is your chance to take an important part in your child's education, so don't miss the opportunity.

SENSORY SMARTS

As your kids get bigger, so can their voices. When they laugh at the dog's antics, it's at top volume. When they call you from the other side of the house, you'd think they had a bullhorn. And the more excited they are to tell you about their day at school, the louder and higher their voices get. They don't realize how loud they are, but if you're sound-sensitive, it may be painful. You need them to lower the volume, but you don't want to dampen their spirits. And you really don't want them to think that you don't want to hear about their day. When they become teenagers they may not be as willing to open up to you, so you want to set the stage for ongoing communication. But how can you cope with their lack of volume control? Headphones and loop-type ear plugs can help. So can raising their awareness of their own noise levels. Consider a nonverbal signal to let them know to reduce their volume. It could be holding your flat hand palm facing downwards and lowering it toward the floor. It could be pantomiming turning down a volume knob. Get their input about the signal that they like best. The main thing is that you and your child both know what it means. When they're younger, make a game of learning the signal. Take turns being the volume controller and the noise maker. The noise maker can either talk or sing or make a repeating sound. The volume controller turns the volume up and down, and the noise maker must make their voice go louder or quieter, following the controller's lead. Have fun with the game, and be sure to let your child be the controller and turn your volume up and down, too. Kids love a game where they can control their parents. Periodically play the game even after they've learned the signal, so that they don't forget. Then, when you have a headache or you're feeling vulnerable to sensory overload, and your child is telling you everything that happened at school at the top of their voice, use the volume controller game to save your senses.

MAKE FAMILY MEETINGS FUN

Now that your kids are in elementary school, they're old enough to be part of the family meetings, which should be fun and fairly short. You can schedule separate parents-only family meetings to discuss boring things like budgets and no-kids-allowed topics like date nights.

The elementary school years are when your kids are old enough to start helping out around the house. If you want to incorporate a system for assigning chores, consider the WORK strategies suggested in *Homeschooling, Autism Style* by Wendela Marsh and Siobhan Marsh (2020, Future Horizons.) WORK stands for Weekly chores, Once-a-day chores, Reinforcement, and Keep it professional.

WORK

Weekly Chores

The W in WORK is for Weekly chores.

Now that your kids are in elementary school, they can start taking on some of the regular chores around the house. Which ones are at their ability level?

Your kindergartener may be happy to put socks over their hands like paws and be a Dusting Bunny, rubbing their sock-paws over surfaces and non-breakable objects that collect dust. (And doesn't everything collect dust?) Crawling under the table to dust the table legs may be a special treat. Want to make it even more fun? Use a permanent marker to draw claws and pads on the socks to make them look even more like a bunny.

Your early elementary kids can probably help put away groceries, fold clean laundry, and even play "Cinderella" and mop the floors. Consider playing a tidying-up scene or song from *Cinderella* or *Enchanted* or *Mary Poppins* as background. Maybe have a whistling contest to see if they can actually whistle while they work. The more fun you can make it, the happier they will be to do their chores. Of course, as they grow older, this may seem too "babyish" and they may prefer an Olympics theme while you provide color commentary and time their tasks.

4: Elementary School

As your kids get closer to the end of their elementary years and closer to middle school, their weekly chores should grow with them. Can they safely use the microwave to help prepare supper for the family? Can they make sandwiches for themselves and their younger siblings? Are they ready to supervise a younger child's chores and provide their own color commentary? You can discuss what chores your kids are ready for, and which ones they actually enjoy, at your Family Meetings. Knowing they're making a contribution to the family is important for growing kids.

Once-a-Day Chores
The O in WORK is for Once-a-day chores.

Daily chores can be exhausting. They're just so daily! Having your kids help you will make a big difference for you, and they'll feel more grown-up knowing they're helping the family. Feeding a pet is a good job for an elementary school child. Foster empathy and care by having a rule that the family doesn't eat dinner until the pets have been fed. They can't feed themselves, so it's up to the humans to make sure they're cared for. Another age-appropriate chore is having your child dry dishes, or load and unload the dishwasher, with supervision if needed. It's so easy to find the kitchen overtaken by dirty dishes, you might want to make a rule that no one watches television or plays a game after dinner until the dishes are washed or in the dishwasher (turned on). With kids to help with the Once-a-day chores, it will be easier to stay on top of things.

Parenting While Autistic

Reinforcement

The R in WORK is for Reinforcement.

We all need reinforcement, whether it's in the form of a paycheck for working, or a smile, hug, and "thank you" for doing something nice for a family member. Kids are no different. If you'd like them to learn the value of money, consider having them earn it through their regular weekly or once-a-day chores. Assign a reasonable dollar amount to each chore. Consider getting your kids' input on this during a Family Meeting. Bear in mind, if the pay rate per job is set too high, they may do just one chore and then feel they can skip the rest because now they're rich. If the pay is too low, they may get discouraged. There's not much you can buy with a quarter these days. This is also a great way for kids to learn the value of coins and dollars if this is something they're studying in math. Practical application with real money is more fun than doing a worksheet about money.

Keep It Professional

The K in WORK is for Keep it professional.

It's a good life skill to learn employability skills at a young age. Once the regular weekly and once-a-day chores have been assigned, there may be other jobs that they may want to take on to earn extra money. In a Family Meeting, come up with a list of extra chores, like washing the car, organizing and wiping down the kitchen cupboards, or helping clean out the garage. Make sure there are age-appropriate jobs for your younger kids as well as bigger jobs for their older siblings. Then keep it professional by having them apply for the job they want. Make a simple application where they have to write their name, the date, the job they want, and why they would be a good person for the job. For instance, they might want the job of giving the dog a bath, and the reason you should hire them is because they get along well with the dog and the dog likes them. After you review the applications, have an interview at a Family Meeting. Ask simple questions, and then hire your child. It's not nepotism; it's real-life skills training. If more than one child wants the same job, rotate it so everyone gets a chance.

Your Family Meetings will be more fun when your kids get to have a voice and feel heard, when they get to make a meaningful contribution to the smooth running of the household, and when they can earn some money for their hard work. It's a win-win-win.

WEEKENDS THAT WORK

As your kids grow up during the elementary school years, their ideas about how they want to spend their weekends might change. Are they on a sports team? Taking music or dance lessons? Learning martial arts or swimming? Suddenly there are more things that keep you busy driving them here and there on the weekends.

If this is difficult for you, you're not alone. All parents struggle at times to keep up with their kids' busy schedules, even if on the outside they look like they've got it all together. When you're a

Parenting While Autistic

neurodivergent parent, though, things that may look simple to others are not so easy for you to cope with. As with everything, advance planning and providing yourself with the accommodations and tools you will need will go a long way.

If you need to go to one game after another, plan to be as comfortable as you can be on the bleachers. You may need an extra cushion, broad brimmed hat, sunglasses, sunscreen, and ear plugs to make the sensory experience endurable. When you can, take turns with your partner or another family member. Kids like to see that someone is there just for them, cheering them on as they play, and if it's sometimes Grandpa and other times an aunt, uncle, or one of their parents, that's okay. When it's not your turn to be there in person, you'll be ready to listen to their play-by-play description of the game after they get home.

If you can't stand the sound of tap shoes on the dance floor, or the smell of chlorine at the pool, or the fluorescent lights in the Tae Kwon Do studio, you can take steps to take care of yourself. When your kids are in the early elementary years, parents may be expected to stay in the waiting room while the children have their lessons. If so, plan on ear plugs to dampen the tap-tap-tap of little dancers, or a face mask with a drop of vanilla between you and the chlorine at poolside as well as a hat and dark glasses, and keep those sunglasses handy indoors if you need them for particularly uncomfortable lighting. If you have a book to read, the other parents are less likely to try to start up a conversation with you if you prefer solitude.

4: Elementary School

As your kids get older, find out from their teachers if it's okay to drop them off at their lessons and then run errands, go home for a bit, or read a book in the car rather than waiting inside. Create some alone time for yourself in the middle of their busy weekends.

Be sure to also make time for family together activities, like a movie night or game night, and for date nights after the kids are asleep. If you plan your weekends in advance so you know what to expect, even a busy family schedule can be manageable.

FICTIONAL FAMILIES

Trish & Bill, Autistic Parents

"We got a letter from Jimmy's school." Trish looked at it without opening it. Just as "Baby James" had become toddler "Jim-Jim," now that he was in grade school their son wanted to be called Jimmy.

"Should we open it?" Bill shared Trish's discomfort around unexpected news, which was often stressful. After a moment, she handed it to him with a sigh.

"You do it."

Bill opened the envelope, slid a form out, and peered at it. "It's about Jimmy," he said.

"I rather thought it would be. Is everything okay? Is he in trouble?"

"Why would he be in trouble? He's a great kid."

"I know, of course he is, but, well, he struggles with some things."

Parenting While Autistic

Bill nodded. "It looks like they want to test him for special education."

"Do they think he's autistic?" With two autistic parents, she wouldn't have been surprised or disappointed, but so far, they hadn't seen any of the autistic features that they had experienced in their childhoods.

"No, it's about reading." At eight years old, their boy was still not reading very well. He could sound out words slowly, but by the time he got to the end of the sentence he had forgotten what it meant. He was discouraged and didn't want to try. If they read something out loud to him, he could understand it, but he just couldn't seem to get it from the page into his brain.

Trish read over his shoulder. "They want our permission to test him. We should sign it. He needs help."

Bill nodded. He wasn't sure how he felt about it, but he trusted Trish. When she made her mind up about something that quickly, then he needed to be right there with her, even if he felt unsure. New things were difficult, and this was all new. "Let's both sign it and send it back, right now."

Trish got a pen and they each signed it, cramming both names onto the parent signature line. They were a team, and whatever their boy needed, they were unified in supporting him.

After the assessment was over, they attended a meeting with the school psychologist, the principal, Jimmy's teacher, and a special education teacher. They learned that Jimmy had a specific learning disability that affected his reading because of his auditory processing.

4: Elementary School

He was as smart as the next kid, which didn't surprise them, but his reading level and his ability to put sounds together into words for phonics were far behind those of other kids his age. His school had a program where the special education teacher would go into his classroom to help several students who needed extra support, and if he needed more help, they could pull him out to work with him separately. However, the school preferred to keep kids in their own classrooms rather than pulling them out. That sounded good to Bill and Trish, too. There were a lot of papers to sign, and finally the meeting was over, just in time for them to pick up Jimmy and drive him home. Trish hesitated at the door before leaving.

"Do you think he could be autistic?" she asked.

"Oh, no," his teacher rushed to say. "We don't think there's anything seriously wrong with Jimmy; he just needs a little help with reading, that's all."

Bill and Trish looked at one another for a moment. Finally, Bill broke the silence.

"We don't believe there is anything seriously wrong with being autistic, since we're both autistic ourselves," he said.

The teacher's face grew pink with embarrassment. "But you don't look—"

The school psychologist interrupted her. "Actually, I was planning to provide staff training in neurodiversity-affirming education this year. Teachers and other staff members will learn that there is nothing wrong with having a different kind of brain. We need to help our neurodivergent students to be themselves and learn in their own way, rather than trying to make them act like everyone else."

"That's right," the principal said. "I guess it's time to get that on the calendar." The psychologist smiled and said she'd get right on it.

Bill and Trish told Jimmy about his new IEP on the way home, and he was fine with it. He already knew the special education teacher and several of the students she worked with, so it didn't seem like a big deal to him. For the rest of his school career, both Trish and Bill showed up to every IEP meeting. They helped the psychologist by giving her feedback on the school neurodiversity training when she asked them, and felt like they were making a positive difference in their son's education. It was a good feeling.

Justin & Maggie, Autistic Dad Adoption Story

"Do you want to stay in the car or go out and grab a cup of coffee? Or you could go home and hang out with your mom and Ray, and then come back and pick me up after the appointment." Maggie placed a hand on Justin's shoulder, and he realized he had been twitching it unconsciously.

"Why would I do that? I want to be with you when we hear what the neurologist has to say."

"You're so fidgety and jittery, I assumed you wanted to get out of here."

"No way, I'm just stimming because I'm nervous, not because I don't want to be here." He took her hand. "We're a team, remember?"

4: Elementary School

"Of course, I do. I just wanted to give you an exit strategy if you needed to escape. I know sitting in waiting rooms is hard for you."

"No need to escape, but thanks." He smiled at her. They had shared similar waiting room experiences with Ray's cardiologist, rheumatologist, pulmonologist; he could hardly remember all the -ologists they'd seen. Even though Ray had a rare syndrome that could cause all kinds of problems, so far his heart, lungs, and joints were doing okay. They wouldn't have to check back in to track his progress for a couple of years. Ray had an IEP as a student with "Other Health Impairment" because of his syndrome, and they loved his IEP team. Things at school were going well, he had a small special classroom, he had friends, and he liked his teachers. Now they were here to find out the results of the neurologist's assessment.

They were called in and sat in two chairs opposite the neurologist behind her large desk, feeling a bit like kids being called into the principal's office.

"So, what's the verdict? Is he autistic? If he is, he got it from me; you know how that runs in families." This was Justin's little joke, since Ray was not biologically related to them.

"He does show a number of autistic characteristics and minimally meets criteria for autism spectrum disorder, severity level 1."

Justin smiled, then tried to cover it up in case it was inappropriate. He felt weirdly happy and almost proud that his boy was autistic, too.

Parenting While Autistic

"But autism is not what's going to get in the way of his future success," the doctor went on. Maggie raised her hand to say something, then quickly put it down, embarrassed.

"So there's something else going on? We already got a clean bill of health on his heart and lungs."

"Ray's cognitive and adaptive scores fall within the lower extreme. Simply put, this describes his ability to learn and his self-help skills, both of which are significantly behind those of same-aged peers."

"We know he needs extra help. But what are you saying, exactly?" Maggie felt a cold fear in her stomach.

"Is he—you know—the 'R' word?" Justin was uncomfortable with suspense or with beating around the bush. He wanted to cut to the results right away.

"No one uses that term anymore; it's become a slur. But both the outdated term 'mental retardation' and the current term 'intellectual disability' refer to a condition involving significant deficits in intellectual function, like reasoning and problem solving, in conjunction with significant deficits in adaptive functioning, such as delays in meeting developmental milestones."

Maggie found her voice first. "We know Ray takes longer to learn than other kids. He was a late talker, and toilet training took a long time. So does this new label just mean he's a slow learner?" She could feel Justin rocking ever so slightly in his chair.

"He has an intellectual disability. At age ten, Ray is functioning at about the level of a six-year-old."

4: Elementary School

Justin flapped a hand slightly, then folded them together. "So, he's four years behind. When he's twenty-four, will he function like a twenty-year-old?"

"It doesn't work like that. Ray will continue to learn throughout his lifetime at his own pace, but the trajectory of his learning will always be lower than that of others his age. He will not 'catch up.' I'm sorry."

"So, what are we supposed to do? How do we help him?" Maggie's voice was shaky, but she sat tall.

"We'll do whatever he needs." Jason put his arm around her shoulder. As well as offering comfort to her, the connection anchored him and helped him regulate.

"Just keep loving him and making sure he's healthy and happy and that his school supports his learning needs." The doctor smiled reassuringly. "You'll all be fine. After all, Ray is exactly the same charming, lovable kid now as he was before you learned these results. Nothing has changed, except you may be better prepared to help him."

"What if we make a mistake? We're not perfect parents." Maggie looked at Justin. "At least, I'm not. I think Justin is the perfect parent for Ray because he understands him so well. I don't know if I'll ever get to that level."

"All parents make mistakes, but children are remarkably resilient. If your intention is to be good and loving parents, little mistakes along the way won't stop him from knowing he is loved and valuable. Just keep going on as you are; you'll all be fine."

Parenting While Autistic

That night after the appointment they brought home Ray's favorite fast food kids' meal with an extra cheeseburger on the side. Even though his appetite had outgrown the kid-sized meal, he still loved the colorful food boxes and the little toys inside. *But*, Justin thought, *what's wrong with that?* He watched Ray delightedly open the toy with his mouth full of French fries, then hand the toy to Maggie to help him put the plastic pieces together. She showed him how they were supposed to fit, and he grinned, thanked her, and took it back to put it together himself. Justin relaxed and smiled. Ray was going to be okay. He was a learner, even if the learning wasn't as fast as the other kids'. But most important, he was a happy and loving boy. There was nothing wrong with their son, and he silently vowed to make sure Ray always knew that.

Lucia & Naima, Two Autistic Moms

"First grade! It's such a big step!" Naima fastened Ruby's hair into puff ponytails with yellow bows. "You are going to look so cute on your first day of school!"

"No, I'm going to look so smart on my first day of school. I'm not going to cute school." Ruby wriggled away as soon as Naima was done and ran upstairs for her new backpack.

"You are so good with her hair," Lucia said. "She looks adorable!"

"I know that's right. But thank God she'd rather be smart than cute!"

4: Elementary School

"That's our girl." They smiled at each other. Ruby had excelled in her private preschool and kindergarten and was ready to start at their neighborhood public elementary school for grades 1–5.

"I can't wait to hear how much her teachers are going to love her when we go to Open House." Naima said. "I used to love Open House, having my parents come see my artwork hanging from the ceiling lights."

"I can't wait to be her Room Mother, like my mom always was when I was in school." Lucia said.

"Excuse me? I'm going to be her Room Mother. You know I make the best cupcakes."

"Well, excuse *me*, but apparently you didn't read the emails, or you'd know that the school only accepts individually wrapped, store-bought treats. I'll be Room Mother, thank you very much."

"Are you pulling rank on me?" Naima looked hurt. "Just because you got to carry her for nine months? I can't believe you'd stoop so low."

"This has nothing to do with being pregnant. I know you would have gone through labor and delivery, but this is just how it turned out. Deal with it."

"I'm supposed to just deal with you trying to steal the joy of being my girl's Room Mother?"

"You were trying to do the exact same thing to me." Lucia paused a moment before the discussion got too heated. "Let's just take a breath. We don't have to decide today. There will be a way for us to share this, just like we share everything. Lovingly."

Parenting While Autistic

Naima reached for her hand and gave it a squeeze. "You're right. This is not a contest. Because if it were a contest, you know I would have won blindfolded with one hand tied behind my back. But it's not."

"No, it is not. We can both win. Let's offer to share the Room Mother duties, fifty-fifty." Lucia smiled. "We've always been a great team, haven't we?"

"We have." Naima reached for her laptop and opened it. "Let's respond to that Room Mother Request email right now, before some greedy Karen gets there first."

For Lucia and Naima, having a united front and sharing equally in the joys and the jobs of motherhood was vital to their relationship and family.

Maria & Santiago, Undiagnosed Autistic Mom

It was finally the day of the twins' First Communion, and Maria did not think she'd ever been so nervous in her life. She had struggled to help the girls prepare and worried so much that she'd put it off until they were eight years old, a year later than usual.

She had done all the things the nuns had told her to do. She'd talked about Jesus and the Eucharist with the girls at home, although she felt uncomfortable, and they didn't seem to take her seriously. She tried to model reverence and focus on the sacrament when taking Communion herself so the girls could learn from her, but the harder she tried, the more awkward she felt. She even tried

4: Elementary School

practicing taking pretend Communion with them at home, but they treated it like a snack and said they wanted more.

Maria had been diligent about taking the girls to Sunday Mass every week, but this was the first time she'd convinced Santiago to come with them. His daughters' First Communion, at least, was important to him, even though he was hardly ever at home anymore.

When the girls had finally taken their first eucharist, she was so relieved it was over, she felt weak and dizzy. She realized she had focused so much on getting the girls fed and ready to go, she had forgotten to eat anything herself. She should go home and eat something. Unfortunately, the priest was not done talking. Maria sat on the hard pew trying to listen while he read more scripture. At least it was in English, rather than the Latin her childhood priest had insisted on.

Her mind latched onto a verse he read from Corinthians: "We shall not all sleep, but we shall all be changed." Rather than grasping the idea of transformation without death, her mind immediately went to the literal meaning of the words. She remembered her little girls when they were babies. *We shall not all sleep, but we shall all be changed.* Babies did not sleep much, but they certainly did need to be changed. The notion tickled her so, she couldn't keep from laughing out loud.

Santiago glared and shushed her, and the girls asked her what was funny.

Parenting While Autistic

"Babies!" she gasped, and then started laughing again. "Babies!" was all she could get out.

Now everyone was staring, and the priest looked at her as if he might have to conduct an emergency exorcism on the spot. People were staring, but she couldn't control it. The harder she tried, the harder she laughed.

Santiago grabbed her arm, pulled her roughly behind him all the way down the aisle and out of the church, and pushed her into the car. The girls climbed silently into the back seat as their mother's laughter turned to quiet weeping. Santiago pulled up in front of their house, and as soon as Maria and the girls got out, he peeled off, leaving them on the sidewalk. Faith and Hope held their mother's hands, and the three walked into the house together.

Maria took a few minutes in the bathroom to recover alone before she came out and made lunch. After the girls ate, she felt the need to explain herself.

"I'm sorry I ruined your first communion." Maria spoke while looking down at her hands. "I was so worried about everything being perfect that I forgot to eat breakfast, and then after you two did everything so well, my nervousness mixed with my happiness and turned into the giggles. You two know what it's like to get the giggles, right?"

"Faith got the giggles in math once, and that gave me the giggles," Hope said.

"No, you got them first and gave them to me!"

4: Elementary School

"Anyway." Maria smiled now, glad her daughters didn't seem mad at her. "I wanted to apologize for taking away from your big moment. Is there anything I can do to make it up to you girls?"

The twins shared one of their trademark 'looks.'

"Can we have ice cream for dinner?"

"Ice cream isn't a dinner food. We still need real dinner." Maria felt bad for shutting them down. "But we could have ice cream in the afternoon, before dinner. How does that sound?"

Maria realized that since the girls were in elementary school and not babies anymore, maybe they could survive knowing that she wasn't the perfect mother. After all, no one is a perfect mother, except for the blessed Mother of God. Her parents had never apologized to her when she was growing up, but she felt good about apologizing to Faith and Hope. She was grateful that they accepted her apology so freely. Not grateful enough to give them ice cream for dinner, but they all three enjoyed an afternoon ice cream party. They had butter pecan with chocolate swirls, and it was delicious.

Robert & Helen, Grandparenting While Autistic

"But I'm telling you, there's nothing wrong with the boy! Bobby is smart as a whip!" Robert felt his temperature rise as he paced back and forth in the kitchen.

"No one's saying there's anything wrong with him." Helen's voice had a calming effect on him.

Parenting While Autistic

"But that quack said he's autistic! Bobby's not some Rain Man. He got a C in math, for heaven's sake." Robert stood behind his chair but wasn't ready to sit back down yet.

Lena waved her hand at her father. "Excuse me, Bobby's mother, sitting right here." She sighed. It was not the first time she and her father had trouble communicating. "This is not about you, Dad. Bobby is my responsibility."

"Well, if you—"

Helen grasped his arm and pulled him down into his chair before he could say something he regretted. She slid his coffee cup closer to him.

"Robert, you need to sit down and drink your coffee. It will keep your mouth occupied." Helen seemed meek to people who didn't know her well, but she could be quietly forceful, and she knew how to get through to Robert when he was being thick-headed.

Robert sipped his coffee and muttered under his breath, "A smoke would keep my mouth occupied, too."

Helen heard him. "Oh, no, you don't. You're not escaping into the back yard with your foul-smelling cigarettes. Lena is here to tell us about Bobby's school testing, and we are here to listen. Quietly."

They did listen quietly, although Robert's brain was going a mile a minute. The more he heard about autism, the more familiar it sounded. Finally, he broke his silence.

"All this stuff that you and that quack are calling autism, that's a bunch of hooey. It's all just normal kid stuff. I was exactly like that when I was a boy, and I'm not autistic." His declaration was

4: Elementary School

met with silence, and he saw his wife and daughter exchange a glance he couldn't interpret. "What? What are you saying? What's going on?"

"Dad, I'm saying my son, Bobby, is autistic, and there's nothing wrong with that. A person can be smart, and loving, and happy, and autistic, all at the same time."

"But he's just like me! How can that be autistic?" He looked at his wife for confirmation. "I mean, autism's just a kid thing, right? They outgrow it?"

"Autistic people don't outgrow who they are. Nobody should be expected to change themselves to fit someone else's idea of 'normal,' whatever that even means." Helen put her hand on Robert's arm. "Lena's been sharing books and articles about autism with me, and I'm learning a lot."

"Well, this is the first I heard of it." Robert stared into his coffee cup, trying to sort out his emotions, which was not his strong suit.

"Dad, I just found out for sure that Bobby is autistic yesterday, and I'm telling you today. I wasn't going to bring it up and start this whole thing until it was confirmed. I knew you would be in denial, and I'm right."

"I'm not 'in denial,' I'm just saying it's not true. Bobby's no more autistic than I am!" Again, the two women glanced at each other. Finally, his wife broke the silence.

"If you believe that all of these autistic features were true for you when you were a boy, and maybe still are today, then maybe you should read some of the things Lena shared with me about autism."

Parenting While Autistic

Helen was usually right, in Robert's experience, and in spite of his confusion, he trusted her as his anchor.

"Well, if you think I should read that stuff, then I guess I will. I'd do anything for Bobby, and if that means learning more about this—" he stopped himself before calling it whackadoodle or horse-feathers— "about this autism, then bring it on."

Robert read everything they brought him, and more. In time he became convinced that he himself was autistic, too. They found a specialist who could test adults for autism, and it was true. Autism was one more thing Robert and Bobby had in common, and there was nothing wrong with that.

Daisy & Crow, Fur-Baby Parents

(Kitty rushes in, slams the door behind her, and flings herself backward against it, arms outstretched, as if pursued by a flight of dragons.)

KITTY: Hurry! She's coming!

DAISY: Hurry where?

CROW: Who's coming?

KITTY: Ms. Markowitz!

DAISY: Miss Whoozitz?

KITTY: Markowitz, my social worker! She wants to put me away!

CROW: Put you away!

DAISY: Never! She'll have to get through us first!

CROW: Where does she want to put you? And why?

KITTY: *(catches her breath)* My dad threw me out. My social worker wants to put me in the system. Which means a foster home, probably full of bullies and pedos and pervs.

4: Elementary School

DAISY: Oh, my!

CROW: I'm not sure I understand.

DAISY: It's from *The Wizard of Oz*, you know, like lions and tigers and bears, only "Bullies and pedos and pervs, oh my!"

CROW: I understood that part. I don't understand why Kitty's social worker is coming here, to our home. Kitty, can you elaborate?

KITTY: ...

CROW: Kitty. What did you tell her?

DAISY: Because whatever you told her, we will back you up 1000 percent!

KITTY: I only need 100.

CROW: We can probably manage 100, but what is it, exactly, that we're backing you up about?

KITTY: I, uh, I told her that you guys wanted to be my foster parents.

CROW: Parents? We're not the parent-type.

DAISY: Is this a trap? Parent trap? Because you said, "parent type," and that sounds like "parent trap," and Kitty's trying to trap us into being her foster parents. You get it, right? I mean, not that you'd have to trap us, Kitty. We're still with you, 1000 percent.

CROW: Why does this social worker think we could be your foster parents? There's probably a lot of legal issues and paperwork and red tape. You'd be better off with experienced, trained foster parents that know what they're doing.

Parenting While Autistic

DAISY: *(under her breath)* … bullies and pedos and pervs, oh my …

CROW: *(whispers back)* I don't think all foster homes are like that.

DAISY: It only takes one, though, doesn't it? If Kitty gets sent to that one-in-a-million foster home that actually is full of bullies and pedos and pervs and we could have prevented it, we'd never forgive ourselves.

KITTY: Please, please, please let me stay with you! My dad doesn't want me, my mom won't stand up to him, and I don't feel safe anywhere else! They'll call me Kevin and probably beat me up worse than my dad.

DAISY: Crow! We have to protect her!

CROW: I know, but what about the legal requirements? There's a whole system we know nothing about. That social worker will take one look at us and know that we're not foster parent material. We need to come up with a plan.

(The doorbell rings.)

KITTY: *(turns slowly to stare at the door in dread)* Too late. She's here.

DAISY: Wait! We can't let her see us! Foster parents are supposed to be grownups!

CROW: We are grownups.

DAISY: …

CROW: …

DAISY: Riiight, I see where you're going with this. *We're* the grownups. That's the ticket. Grownups. Okay, that's our story, now we all have to stick to it!

4: Elementary School

(The doorbell rings again, followed by a knock.)

DAISY: Do we have to answer it?

CROW: Take a breath. We can do this. *(puts hand on doorknob, hesitates, then suddenly flings the door open just as Sandra Markowitz is about to knock, throwing her off balance)*

SANDRA: Sorry! *(manages to stop herself before she knocks on Crow's face)*

CROW: Come in. You must be the social worker.

SANDRA: Yes, I'm Sandra Markowitz. Are you Kevin's …

CROW: Kitty's.

SANDRA: *(turns the page on the file in her hands)* Oh! Yes, I'm sorry, Kitty. So, are you Kitty's parents? I mean, this was the address I was given, but … who are you?

DAISY: We're her parents.

CROW: —friends! We're her friends.

DAISY: Her parents' friends.

CROW: No, just Kitty's friends.

DAISY: We're just Kitty's friends. She's been staying with us.

CROW: She said it was okay with her parents. I should have called them.

DAISY: We should have called them. But we hate talking on the phone. Well, mostly me.

CROW: Sorry, Ms. Markowitz. I'm Crow, and this is my wife, Daisy. So, why are you here, exactly? What can we do for you?

DAISY: Because we'll do anything for Kitty.

SANDRA: Well, our first priority is to reunify families rather than separating them.

Parenting While Autistic

KITTY: You know my parents don't want me. I can't go back there.

SANDRA: *(reads further in her file)* Yes. I have their statement. I'm so sorry, Kitty.

KITTY: Can't I just be emancipated and not have any parents?

SANDRA: You'd have to be fully self-supporting. Do you have a job?

DAISY: She's our dog walker.

SANDRA: Does she earn enough to be considered fully self-supporting as a dog walker?

CROW: *(sighs)* No, not really.

DAISY: We mostly pay in pizza.

CROW: But we're happy to have her stay here with us.

SANDRA: She's a minor; she needs to be placed in a foster home.

KITTY: Where are you sending me?

SANDRA: *(turns another page in her file, looks back and forth between pages, then closes the file)* Nowhere. We don't have any available foster placements.

CROW: So her parents don't want her, and you don't have a foster family for her. What happens now?

SANDRA: Well, Kitty seems comfortable with you two.

KITTY: Totally!

SANDRA: So if you two apply to be a resource family for her, I can expedite the paperwork.

DAISY: Yes, please! Expedite!

CROW: Whatever you need from us, we'll do it. Kitty's been like part of our family.

4: Elementary School

DAISY: And now she really will be family! *(hugs Kitty)*
(Sandra leaves, promising to email the necessary forms and information.)
KITTY: I thought you guys never wanted to have kids?
DAISY: Babies. We never want to have babies.
CROW: Luckily, you're not a baby. Just call us Mom and Parent.
KITTY: Uh, thanks, but I'm just going to call you Daisy and Crow.
DAISY: Kids! They grow up so fast!
(Thus, the Daisy and Crow Forever Home grows to a family of four: Daisy, Crow, Bugbear, and now Kitty. Just weird enough to be perfect.)

PARENT TO PARENT

"When our children were of age to begin grade school, I discontinued my part-time employment at our local bank and started a home daycare. We wanted to raise our own children but thought it might be a good idea to have a companion or two as they grew. My children did well with their companions, but there were a few bullies at the home daycare. My kids knew how to respect others, but I did not know what to do about this sudden change, this bullying behavior that I was not familiar with. I wish now that I had confronted the other parents about the behaviors of their children. If we could only have the wisdom that we have in our sixties, transferred to our young ignorant minds of our twenties.

"I bought a book about raising boys as my two sons grew (*The Conscious Parent's Guide to Raising Boys: A Mindful Approach to Raising a Confident, Resilient Son*, by Cheryl L. Erwin and Jennifer

Parenting While Autistic

Costa, 2017, Adams Media.) I also became the PTA president, a parent advocate for the school district, and the block club leader. I wanted to create a perfect neighborhood for the children."

— James, late-diagnosed autistic dad

"I'm not the most nurturing type of parent, but I found a good 'workaround' by using my organizational abilities to support my kids' social lives by organizing various social events and volunteering at their favorite summer camp. Using the skills I do have to come alongside my kids' activities worked really well for me. I couldn't be the mom who would sit and braid your hair and talk about boys, but I could be the mom who ran summer camp so you could sit around with other people who could braid your hair and talk about boys."

— Krista, autistic mom

Chapter 5

Middle School

Smells Like Tween Spirit

"There's something incredibly vulnerable about middle school ... We're really impressionable during that period. The cement's still wet, so to speak, and a lot of things later in life are born during that season."

— Mat Kearney, American musician

"Conscious parenting is not about being perfect, it's about being aware. Aware of what your kids need from you to reach more of their full potential."

— Alex Urbina, author

5: Middle School

The middle school years are such an important and difficult time of life. Your kids still have one foot in elementary school and one foot already in high school, hovering between. One moment they're acting like goofy kids, and the next minute they're too mature to be seen with anyone as uncool as their parents. The goofy kid embarrasses you, acting like a gangly colt or a hyper puppy running up and down the supermarket aisles. The mature teen is embarrassed by your very existence, since they're clearly too sophisticated to need parenting. All around, it's an embarrassing time of life.

It is particularly unfortunate that so many school systems isolate children at these vulnerable ages in middle schools. All the students in middle school are going through the same confusing roller coaster. There are no older kids to emulate, no little kids to be an example for. Everyone is in that same place, not a child any longer, but nowhere near being an adult. If your tweenager has the option of attending a K–12 school with students ranging all the way from kindergarten through twelfth grade, they will have the advantage of perspective, seeing where they've been and where they're going in the students around them. Even a K–8 followed by high school may be easier on kids in grades 5–8 than a traditional middle school experience.

However, if your child needs to attend a separate middle school, the experience can still be a positive one. When parents are observant, they can alert the school to a potential issue before it becomes a big problem. Autistic parents are among the most observant people I

Parenting While Autistic

know, with strong attention to detail. They are perfectly poised to recognize behavioral changes when something is wrong with their child and can reach out to their child and, if needed, to their child's teacher for support.

If your child is autistic, too, you're probably well aware of the high rate of suicide among autistic teens. The good news is they have you. Having an autistic parent who truly understands their unique brain is an incredible gift for an autistic child. You survived middle school as an autist, whether or not you had a diagnosis at the time. This puts you in the best position to act as a buffer between your child and the world. Be their safety zone. Knowing that you love them unconditionally is a powerful force against depression and suicidal ideation. If your child experiences this, find them a neurodiversity-affirming therapist to help them learn effective coping strategies. It's important that any professionals you choose for your family not only are accepting of diversity, but also truly believe there is nothing wrong with being autistic other than the challenges of living in a neuro-majority world. Your child's counselor should never try to make them change or pretend to be "normal," as that denial of who they really are can be harmful. But I don't need to tell you that. You have lived as an autistic person and are well aware of how it feels when someone tries to force you to mask in order to look like everyone else.

These years can be baffling to everyone in the family. Your tween keeps bouncing between being a little kid and a teenager. It's difficult to follow. Autistic parents who prefer familiarity over change may feel particularly challenged. How can you maintain your own equilibrium while your child seems to be in constant flux?

It's important to remember who they are and where they're going.

WHO THEY ARE

Who is that annoying mid-sized person living in your home? They started out as your precious baby, your bundle of joy, a charming little being filled with love, curiosity, and delight in the world. Yes, that hormonal whirlwind is the self-same child you've always adored, still do, and always will.

WHERE THEY'RE GOING

Your time of living together is finite and part of a bigger human pattern. First, you lived a life before they were born. Second, you are now living a life together, parent and children under the same roof. Third, in the distant future, they will go on living their lives after your death.

But there is a space between second and third, like the infield on a baseball diamond. This is the time after your children lived with you and before you die: the time of the Empty Nest. Depending on many different variables, most of them financial, your children may or may not move out on their own. If they do, you will experience the empty nest with its pros and cons. We'll talk more about this in chapter nine, but for now, let's just remember that this is the direction they're headed: out into their own independent lives.

WHAT TO REMEMBER

While they are at their peak of being both confused and confusing, annoyed and annoying, embarrassed and embarrassing, it's helpful to remember who they are (your sweet baby) and where they're going (off to give you an empty nest).

As a strategy to keep your balance during these years, find your favorite baby picture of your little darling, and put it where you can see it every day. It might be on your mirror, or your phone, or the refrigerator, or in your wallet. This will remind you of who they are.

Alongside that, find or draw an image of a nest with no eggs—an empty nest. This will remind you that your time with them living in your home may be limited. You may one day have an empty nest. If this idea sounds good to you, then let the picture remind you that you can make it through the teen years and regain your quiet and calm nest. If the idea of an empty nest makes you feel lonely, it could remind you to appreciate them while they're still here, so that you might find patience in the chaos. If the idea of an empty nest makes you too sad, though, don't put up a picture of a nest. If it's not helpful to you, don't do it. Find a picture of a beach, or an Italian villa, or any dream vacation you'd like to go on when you don't have kids in tow.

5: Middle School

AND FINALLY...

You will get through these years. Your middle schooler will survive and be transformed into a high schooler. As an autistic parent, your heightened sense of awareness and observation will help you notice changes in your child's mood or attitude. There will probably be times of stress or depression or anxiety along with the times of fun and exploration and curiosity. Even if you don't know exactly what the changes mean for them, you can ask. Let them know you care and that you are there if they want to talk about what's going on in their lives. Keep that communication avenue open during the middle school years to help ensure ongoing communication during the high school years.

Despite the many changes, the emotional highs and lows, and the trials of testing the limits that make up the middle school years, there's more. You will laugh, you will enjoy their company, you will be proud of them. One day they'll be grown and you may see them as a friend and equal, and you'll look back together fondly at all of the memories you are making right now.

LIKES, PUBERTY, AND THE PURSUIT OF FLAPPINESS

Likes: Social Media

Chances are, your middle school child spends a lot of time looking at screens, whether it's a phone, tablet, computer, or television. It's not just your child, it's their generation and the other generations, older and younger. We live in a world of screens, for better or for worse.

For better is when they use their screens to read, study, and learn, to follow their passions, and to connect with peers. Playing video games can provide a much-needed time of relaxation after a stressful day at school. It's your right to know what your kids are using their screens for, and you'll want to track a couple of things.

Are their games helping them relax by letting them build things, plant and harvest crops, interact with cartoon animals, or explore the world of nature, civilization, the ocean, or outer space? Are they chatting with friends who help them feel better about themselves? Are they learning things that enrich and inspire them?

Or are their games making them tense as they fight with monsters, shoot, crash cars? Are they following peers who criticize them and make them feel worse about themselves? Will they do crazy and possibly dangerous stunts just to get "likes?" Are they reading about things that worry them and increase their anxiety?

5: Middle School

You can tell a lot by observing them while they're online and after they shut off the screen. Do they seem relaxed while playing or hunched over with an anxious expression? Do they laugh or cry when they read what others have written to or about them? Is someone cyber-bullying or trolling them, or are they doing this to others? Do they leave their screen filled with worried questions about potential natural disasters or political problems that keep them awake at night? Do they have a lot of trouble turning off their screens, so that you suspect they may be addicted? If you see significant negative reactions or anxious behaviors that seem related to screen time, you may need to have a talk with them. Discuss what is and is not appropriate or uplifting and what can be harmful. If they are being bullied online, seek out a counselor for them who is experienced with this issue.

Puberty: You Knew It Was Coming, and Now it's Here

It's never easy to talk to your kids about puberty, their changing bodies, and sexual topics. Children are maturing physically at a younger age than in the past, so you don't want to wait to have "The Talk." If you have difficulty communicating socially about uncomfortable topics, consider finding a book at the library to help. Find out what the school covers on the topic. Talk to their pediatrician or primary care nurse practitioner if you need health and wellness advice. Don't ignore puberty; it won't just go away quietly. Better to prepare yourself and bring it up as a conversation.

Parenting While Autistic

Your child may not admit that they have questions, but if you leave a book about puberty lying around the house, they may pick it up and read it. Then you can ask if they have any questions and open the door for discussion.

The Pursuit of Flappiness: Why Not?

You may be someone who finds that flapping your hands, rocking, or engaging in other "stimming" activities is helpful to your mental health and wellbeing. Many people "stim" to relax, self-regulate, or express their feelings. If it feels good to flap, I hope you feel free to do what works for you.

Now that you have a middle schooler, though, you may have noticed that they seem embarrassed by your flappiness. You might be tempted to mask, trying to force yourself not to move your body in the ways that feel right to you. Of course, to mask or not to mask is always your own choice. Sometimes masking can be a useful survival strategy. It can be incredibly exhausting, though.

When you make your own decision about whether to mask to avoid embarrassing your middle schooler, just remember: They will be embarrassed by you anyway. All middle schoolers are embarrassed by the very existence of their parents. It is natural for this age group. So bear this in mind. You may still choose to stifle your stims, such as when your kids have friends visiting, or you may choose to normalize stimming by just being yourself. If your child has big feelings about it, do give them the respect of listening to them and hearing them out, and then make your own choice to flap or not to flap.

5: Middle School

SENSORY SMARTS

I don't know what is more sensory-overwhelming than the sounds and smells of a pre-teen or tweenager. You'll become intimately familiar with the odor of sweaty gym suits, hormonal body odor, fruity-flowery hair and skincare products, and overpowering colognes. To survive these smelly years with the fewest episodes of sensory overload, you'll need two things: Procedures and Protection.

Procedures for Smells

If you have procedures in place, you can nip the sensory onslaught in the bud. To prevent some of the worst smells of the middle school years, establish procedures for certain tasks to be completed on a regular basis. Create visual schedules for what must be done so that you don't have to keep reminding them—just point to the schedule, no nagging required. Here are some of the smells of the tween years and procedures to handle them.

Gym Clothes

As soon as your kids are ready, teach them to do their own laundry. Then make it a rule that as soon as they get home on Friday, the gym clothes go straight into the washer before they start their after-school routines of snacking and decompression time. If they're not ready to learn how to operate the washer and dryer, or if you use a laundromat outside of your home, then teach them to put the clothes into the appropriate laundry basket, rather than spending the weekend in the backpack. You don't want to be the one to unzip that pack if they've forgotten to take them out to wash.

Old Food

The remains of that half-eaten tuna sandwich, banana peels, food wrappers, and apple cores make for a potent odor when they've spent time in a backpack, in pockets, or behind your kid's bed or desk. Schedule daily food and trash checks, focusing on the places these smells are most likely to be forgotten. Daily backpack checks will also bring to light forgotten homework, notes, and permission slips. The responsibility of these food, trash, and backpack checks should be your child's, not yours. You don't want to find those surprises, and they need to learn to manage their own stuff.

Body Odor

Kids at this age are notoriously poor at personal hygiene. If this is true for yours, consider writing up and posting in their bathroom the procedures for staying sweet-smelling instead of stinky. Make sure they know that a shower means the water has to actually hit their body and that soap must be used liberally. Consider posting a reminder that when a shampoo bottle is empty, they need to throw it away and get out a new one or put it on the grocery list. If they keep refilling the empty bottle with water, it's not going to be effective. Brushing teeth twice a day may require a reminder note on the mirror. If your child is autistic, too, you'll understand that they need to find the hygiene products that smell and feel right to them, and keep buying the same ones rather than switching brands.

Overdone Cologne

The first time a tweenager has access to cologne or body spray, the tendency is usually to overdo it. More is better, right? Wrong. If a parent is autistic and has a sensitivity to chemical perfumes, it may be intolerable even in smaller doses. If anyone in the family has an olfactory sensitivity, a family procedure might be that no new smells come into the house unless everyone agrees it is acceptable. You can take a family trip to a scented body care product store and let everyone take a sample sniff before agreeing on a cologne for regular use in the house. Many such stores offer small sample strips of cardboard that a small amount of a sample can be sprayed on. That way, if someone in the family cannot tolerate being inside the store, a small sample can be carried outside to them for the sniff test. Then, once your tweenager has a smell-sensitivity-approved cologne, teach them how much to use (which is not very much at all.) If it's in a spray, it's usually a good idea to spray a small amount (not more than one spray) into the air and then walk forward into the scent, rather than spraying it directly onto themselves.

Protections for Smells

While having procedures and schedules in place can be effective in preventing some of the olfactory sensory assault that tweens can provide, it's not always enough. Sometimes you need protection from the inevitable smells that are going to happen regardless of your pre-planned procedures. That's when you need protection.

Competing Scents

Some people find that using a room freshener spray or plug-in device can hold its own against the odors that seem to take hold in a tweenager's home. Others find that burning a scented candle is effective and recommend natural soy candles. Test them before you commit to them, though. You don't want the remedy to be worse than the problem.

Masking Scents

Some people find that putting a small amount of their favorite scent on the inside of a face mask is a good personal solution for temporary overpowering odors. Vanilla extract and essential oils can provide a pleasant aroma. People who don't enjoy the feeling of wearing a face mask any longer than they need to might put a little scented lotion on their face, especially right under their noses, or hold a scented object or handkerchief near their nose as needed.

Even though there is a lot of sensory input going on during the middle school years, with a little creativity and planning, you will survive.

5: Middle School

MAKE FAMILY MEETINGS FUN

Now more than ever before, you'll want to include your child in your Family Meetings. Ask them what they want to talk about, and put their ideas on the agenda. Really listen when they bring things up. This is when they can negotiate for a later bedtime, increased screen time, or a higher allowance. Let them bring it up at the Family Meeting, and then really listen to their reasons for asking for extra privileges. It's easy to fall back on that old standby, "No, because I'm your parent," and its partner, "I'm not your friend's parent, so their bedtime/screen time/allowance is none of my business." Consider their requests respectfully.

Be prepared to make a change when appropriate, such as giving them an extra half hour before bedtime as long as they have no trouble getting themselves up for school in the morning. Of course, if they rely on you to remind them again and again to get up and get ready, then they are demonstrably not yet mature enough for a later bedtime. Have a stipulation that for every morning that you have to ask them to get up more than once or that they are not out of bed independently by a certain time, their bedtime that night will revert to the earlier time. Each morning that they get up easily with no extra reminders needed, that night they can have the later bedtime. If they want to stay up later, they need to show you that they can handle it by getting up easily in the morning. By the same token, if they want a higher allowance, they should be ready to take on extra chores around the house.

Parenting While Autistic

Your Family Meeting is a great place for your middle-school-aged children to learn about communication, negotiation, and responsibility.

WEEKENDS THAT WORK

One thing about middle schoolers is that they are old enough to want to spend even more time hanging out with their friends or doing their own thing, but they're still not old enough to drive. At the same time, they're young enough to have fun doing the weekend family things you've always done together, even though they're old enough to be embarrassed by it.

Can you plan weekends as a family despite having a hard-to-please, middle-of-the-road tween? Yes, you CAN, with Choices, Alternatives, and Negotiations.

CAN

Choices
The C in CAN is for Choices.

Whenever possible, let your middle schooler choose a weekend activity for the family. Would they rather watch a movie with the family, go to the park for a picnic, or go to a roller rink or skate park together as a family excursion? Give them a limited number of choices that you'd be happy to agree to. Then, give them even more

5: Middle School

choices, so they feel like the weekend plan is really theirs and not imposed on them by their parents. Movie night at home? Let them choose which film to stream. A picnic? Let them choose the park or the menu. Family hike? Let them choose which foods to pack for lunch. Rotate whose turn it is to choose, because they live in a family and everyone wants to have a turn to choose. Having a choice, and accepting that other people have choices, too, is important for preteens and tweens.

Alternatives

The A in CAN is for Alternatives.

Sometimes a decision is made for them and they don't have a choice. You can take some of the sting out by offering a few alternatives within the scope of the weekend choice that you've already made. If you've already chosen a movie, let them choose a dinner menu or snacks. Challenge them to come up with a theme that goes with the movie. They might even help prepare it.

If they can't opt out of a picnic at the park with their younger siblings, consider relaxing any rules you might have about putting down the phone or gaming device during meals. Let them play or text their friends while the younger kids play on the equipment and the parents have a quiet conversation of their own.

If you're all going shopping together, you might let them choose another department of the store to browse in, such as clothing or music, while you take the younger kids to the toy aisle. Make sure they are clear about any rules you set for how long they can shop on their own and being reachable if you need to contact them quickly.

When they have to go along on a family outing that was not of their choosing, at least having a few alternatives will let them feel less like a little kid and more like the middle schooler they are.

NEGOTIATION
The N in CAN is for Negotiation.

If they want to have more choices and alternatives than they've had in the past, let them bring up their preferences for weekend activities at a Family Meeting. They can negotiate for their preferences. Listen and respect them. Remember, they are learning to be adults from the way they see you manage disagreements by negotiating conflicts. If you must say no to their requested weekend plans because of safety or financial issues, tell them why. Just knowing that you heard them and considered their preferences is a positive step forward in the teen years.

FICTIONAL FAMILIES

Trish & Bill, Autistic Parents

"Jim hasn't picked out any valentines for school yet." Trish was making a grocery list. She was proud of how their boy had grown, insisting on being called Jim instead of Jimmy now that he was in middle school.

"Isn't he a bit old for that?" Bill asked, looking up from his crossword puzzle.

5: Middle School

"They have some with superheroes on them," she said. "They don't look babyish. But he keeps telling me he doesn't want me to buy any at all."

"I guess he doesn't want to hand out valentines, then."

"I'm worried that he'll be embarrassed when all of the other kids walk around the room, dropping their valentines into the boxes on their desks. How will it look if he just sits there with no valentines to give?"

"Do they still do that in middle school?" Bill asked.

"Don't they? I don't remember." Trish had a hard time remembering her middle school years, when the mean girls had turned on her. Thank goodness they didn't have mean girls at her college.

"They have different classes and teachers now. They might not make valentine boxes anymore. Did you get a note home asking you to send in a shoe box to decorate this year?"

"No, there was nothing about it on the parent email this month, or on the school website. I just assumed they already had enough boxes for everyone."

Bill put down his crossword puzzle book and pen and looked deep in thought. "I don't know, I was just remembering ..." He trailed off.

"Remembering what?"

"My worst Valentine's Day ever. The year I didn't get a single valentine from anyone."

"That's terrible! I can't believe your teacher would let that happen! It's so cruel." Trish felt overcome by sadness for her husband, as piercing as if it had happened to her, and only yesterday instead of years ago.

"My teacher didn't give me a valentine, either. I was heartbroken."

"Did you ever find out why that happened?"

"Well, yes. I told my mom that night, and she said that was one of the differences between elementary school and middle school. In elementary school, everyone gave valentines to everyone, and the teacher let kids decorate boxes and sent home a list with everyone's name so no one would be left out."

"Which is as it should be."

"But not in middle school. Kids are older; they move from class to class and teacher to teacher. Passing out valentine cards to everyone is a kid thing, not a middle school thing." He smiled sheepishly. "When my mom pointed this out, I realized that I hadn't seen anyone else get valentines, either. It wasn't just me."

"Oh." Trish thought for a moment. "I guess our boy knows more about middle school than his mother." She crossed out valentines on her shopping list.

"He's growing up." Bill smiled at her. "But we can still have a valentine's celebration at home, with chocolates. He's not about to outgrow chocolates, is he?"

Trish smiled. "No, he is not. I'll add chocolate to the grocery list instead of valentine cards."

Trish learned to trust that her son knew what was going on at his school, and they all enjoyed the chocolates.

5: Middle School

Justin & Maggie, Autistic Dad Adoption Story

"Tell me again about the special classroom options?" Justin was exhausted by the social demands of the IEP meeting with a table full of professionals across from them, as well as by the sensory overload of the buzzing fluorescent lights and somebody's perfume. He longed to escape, but he knew this was important to Ray's future.

"We recommend 100-percent inclusion into the general education program for all of our students. That way they can be with their same-aged peers but still learn at their own pace."

"So you have him sit in an algebra or geometry class, but he does worksheets on addition and subtraction, because that's what he can do?"

"Well, yes, he can do that."

"What about history? He sits in a class where the other kids are working with a textbook he can't begin to read while he colors a picture of the Liberty Bell?" He felt his hands vibrating and folded them to avoid stimming in public, and he relaxed a bit when Maggie placed a hand gently on his arm.

"He may not be prepared to engage in the classroom discussions or essay writing, but he can still be there, with his friends."

"Is his algebra teacher going to teach him how to count money, or is his English teacher going to teach him how to read at the third-grade level? Or will he just sit there?"

Maggie spoke up. "I think our concern here is that he will be left behind. It seems like no one will be actually teaching him, except for an aide who is not a trained teacher, and a special teacher checking in occasionally. They'll just be letting him sit in the regular classrooms while they teach the rest of the kids."

The IEP team looked at each other uncomfortably. "We hate to take students away from their friends and isolate them in separate classrooms."

Maggie looked at Ray's current special teacher from the elementary school. "Who are Ray's friends now?" The teacher listed several special education students, so Maggie pressed on. "Does he have any friends in the regular classes, or are all of his friends kids who are like him, who are learning at their own pace in the special class?" They learned that Ray had good friends in the special class, but he did not play with kids from the general ed classes on the playground, preferring his friends in the smaller, special class.

Justin spoke up again. "When I was a kid, I was ostracized by the other kids. I had no friends. I didn't know then that I was autistic, but the other kids knew I was different, and they had nothing to do with me, except when they were bullying me." He took a deep breath. "I don't want that for Ray. I read a study where autistic people have no social communication problems when they're with other autistic people, only when they're trying to talk with so-called 'normal' people. So I want Ray's middle school placement to be in a specialized classroom with other kids like him. Can we do that?"

It turned out that they could do that with parent permission, or in this case parent insistence. The IEP team arranged for Ray to start middle school in the Special Day Class (SDC) rather than in the general education or "mainstream" inclusion program.

5: Middle School

When he got there on the first day of school, he saw that several of his friends from elementary school were in his class. Ray had a great learning experience in middle school, thanks to his parents advocating for him.

Lucia & Naima, Two Autistic Moms

"I finally got Ruby to open up a window and air out her room. I don't know why her art supplies have to be so stinky." Lucia sat down beside her wife, happy to have a moment together now that their daughter was upstairs for the night.

"Her art supplies aren't the only stinky things. Did you get her to shower?"

"Yes, finally. She always has one more thing she has to do first."

"She's always been a busy kid." Naima smiled. "Say, did you notice how she was acting at the restaurant tonight?"

"She ordered chicken tenders and mac and cheese, like always." Naima thought about their dinner out to celebrate her graduating from sixth grade to seventh grade. "How do you mean?"

"Well, she kept her head down, she barely said a word to us, and she sighed loudly at irregular intervals. Something was going on, right? That's not normal for her, is it?" As an autistic mom, Lucia sometimes worried about her parenting awareness.

"Oh, yeah, you're right." Naima nodded. "I think she was probably just embarrassed to be seen with us."

"You're kidding!" Lucia was taken aback. "Because she has two moms? Or because we're autistic?"

Parenting While Autistic

"I don't think so. I think it's just a normal thing for middle schoolers to be embarrassed by having parents."

"I was never embarrassed by my parents. If we were in public, I always wanted to be right beside them."

"I don't remember being embarrassed by my parents, specifically; I was just constantly embarrassed at that age."

"So, as autistic tweens we weren't embarrassed by our parents, but Ruby is embarrassed by us? She's so typical. I keep forgetting."

"Yeah, she may be in the minority as a mixed-race daughter of lesbians, but she is definitely in the neuro-majority." Naima wondered what it must feel like to be in the majority of any group. "It seems weird, doesn't it?"

"Yeah, it does." Lucia sighed. "It's like her whole life I've been waiting for her autistic features to kick in, but they never have."

"I don't think they're going to. I believe what we have here is a neurotypical daughter."

"How are we supposed to raise a typical child when we've never been typical ourselves?"

Naima put her arm around her wife. "Just the way we've been doing it so far. By loving her and encouraging her to be herself. Whoever that is."

"So, you believe we can be the best parents for her?"

"Believe it? I've seen it with my own eyes!" She gave Luisa a side hug. "You worry a lot, but you are an amazing mom. Ruby's lucky to have you."

"And you." Luisa relaxed. "We make a good team, don't we?"

5: Middle School

"Yes, we do. I promise you, Ruby will survive her middle school years, and so will we."

And they did.

Maria & Santiago, Undiagnosed Autistic Mom

The day finally came when Santiago stopped coming home at all. Maria received divorce papers and signed them without reading them. She had never missed him when he stayed out all night. Now that she had her girls, her sweet twins, she saw no reason to have a husband taking up space in her bed. She was relieved to be spared his horrible sleeping sounds, snoring all night, and those smacking mouth noises he made when he woke up. She felt her anxiety decrease now that he wasn't constantly underfoot, watching her, judging her. What a blessed relief to have him gone!

She thought about her new situation as a single mother. Santiago was very good at sending money for her and the girls every month, even before the divorce paperwork, so she wouldn't have to get a job. She'd never had a job, and she didn't think she'd be good at anything. She was grateful to him for that.

Now, though, a new anxiety rose up: the fear of losing her girls. She heard that he had a new woman in his life. Would they try to take custody away from her? With younger children it was common for them to stay with their mother, but now they were in middle school. If a judge asked them who they wanted to live with, what would they say?

Parenting While Autistic

Maria knew she had to step up and be the best possible parent she could be. They deserved it, and she couldn't bear the thought of them leaving her. But how does one go about learning to be the perfect parent? Her mother was no longer able to come and help her as she had when the girls were born.

Maria headed to the library to read every parenting book she could get her hands on. When her mother asked her what she wanted for birthdays or Christmas, it was always books and magazines about parenting. Maria soaked in information like a sponge and put it to good use. How could she fashion herself into a capable single mother?

First, she had to know what children needed at this age. Middle school had been a muddle for Maria. She hoped and believed that her awful experience would not be the fate of her girls. For one thing, she had always been alone, and Faith and Hope would always have each other. Twins seemed like such a novelty that other girls tended to gravitate to their cafeteria table and want to be their friends, so Maria wouldn't have to worry about the social part of their lives. She'd leave that to them, since she herself had been such a dismal failure at social events and trying to make friends.

What else did girls this age need?

First, kids needed to know that they were loved unconditionally. Maria certainly loved Faith and Hope with all her heart. But did they know? She had never been very good at communicating, especially when it came to talking about feelings. She decided to make a rule for herself that she would say "I love you" every morning as they

5: Middle School

left for school and every night as they went to bed. It wasn't enough for her to feel loving toward them; she had to let them know in so many words that they were loved.

Second, she had to keep them alive. Children need to eat. She couldn't get lost in her thoughts or in a book and forget to feed them, and she had to make sure there were healthy snacks in the house at all times. That meant getting organized.

Third, they needed a clean and orderly home. That was her job, too. She knew that lots of kids this age helped out with chores and housework, but she wasn't ready to give up her role as sole house-keeper. Doing the cooking and cleaning was a tangible way that she showed her love for her daughters.

Fourth, they needed plenty of sleep at this age. She would have to be strict about bedtimes. She wasn't used to being strict with them, but she knew this was important.

Fifth, they needed structure and rules. They had to know what was acceptable and what was not, and they needed reasonable consequences for breaking rules. She couldn't just let them be their own parents and do whatever they wanted, even though she suspected they might do a better job than she would. But she knew she could get better, and she worked hard to prove herself worthy of being their mother.

Maria threw herself into becoming a model parent whole-heartedly. She made lists and schedules for herself. She would need systems to help her keep track of everything.

Parenting While Autistic

Her first system helped her make sure they knew they were unconditionally loved. Maria didn't want to forget to tell them she loved them, so she taped a baby picture of the girls onto her mirror. When she was getting ready for the day or getting ready for bed, she would see it and remember how much she loved them. If she hadn't yet told them, she'd go right then and say, "I love you." She also put "I love you" notes in their lunch sacks. At first, she drew a heart and wrote it on the outside of the sack, but they were embarrassed. Then she put it on their napkins, but the ink got on their hands and faces. Another fail! Finally, she just put little sticky notes on their sandwich baggies so they could read them but then leave them inside the sack so no one else would see.

Her second system helped her keep them alive and nourished. Maria knew she would need a meal organization system, because she felt that she was naturally disorganized and forgetful. She bought kitchen timers and labeled them for the different things she wanted to remember to do. One timer reminded her to make a good hot breakfast, seven days a week. Another timer told her when it was time to start dinner, and she had another for packing their lunches the night before. She knew that she could have just reset a single timer for each of these things, but for her it was important to have a different color of timer, with the job and the time written on it with indelible ink. She couldn't have dreamed that by the time her daughters were in college she'd be using a phone for all her lists, schedules, and reminder alarms. A phone! Imagine!

5: Middle School

Each week Maria made and froze batches of sandwiches and baggies of cookies, easy to toss into their lunch sacks with a piece of fruit. She made a regular weekly grocery list that stayed the same with all of the things that she knew they would run out of, like milk, eggs, bread, fruit, and toilet paper. She could add other things to the list as they came up, but she wouldn't have to work at remembering the staples. Maria also made weekly menus with the same suppers each day of the week, such as Macaroni Monday, Taco Tuesday, and Stew Saturday. When her girls complained about the repetition and wanted variety, she added more weekly menus and cycled through them so that they didn't have the same menu two weeks in a row. Lists and kitchen timers ruled her life and reduced her anxiety. She wouldn't have to rely on her own memory or time management if she had a system in place.

Her third system helped her keep a clean and orderly home. Maria read about housework tips and strategies and put some of them in place. Her favorite housekeeping tips were from the Sidetracked Home Executives, two sisters who had overcome their own messiness by getting organized. Maria followed their advice. She got 3x5 cards and an index box. She wrote a job on each card, such as "Sweep the kitchen" or "Launder the sheets and towels." Each day after the girls were off to school, she went to her box and pulled out the card at the front and did that job. Then the card went back to the back of the box. After she finished her jobs for the morning, she would do something she enjoyed, such as having

Parenting While Autistic

a cup of coffee at the kitchen table, looking out the window, and enjoying the way the wind moved the leaves.

Her fourth system helped her make sure the girls got enough sleep. Maria knew from her parenting books that kids in their early teens actually might need even more sleep than they did in elementary school. Unfortunately, this happens right when they want to be more grown-up, which to them means staying up later. It wouldn't be easy for her to enforce a strict bedtime with them. They were good kids, and they loved staying up and talking and giggling together. Maria decided to let them help her with this.

At their next Family Meeting, Maria told Faith and Hope that, now that they were in middle school, they should help make some of the decisions, like their bedtimes. They were thrilled and wanted to stay up until midnight every night, but that wasn't what Maria had in mind. She asked them to take a poll among their friends and write down everyone's bedtimes to see how late others their age were staying up. Then, at their next family meeting, they reviewed the information collected. Maria discarded the one who said they stayed up until 3:00 AM as either untrue or evidence of poor parenting, and the girls didn't object. Then they took an average of the remaining times. The result was a half hour later than their previous bedtime. She asked them if they thought they could get up and be ready for school if they stayed up that late, and they eagerly agreed. However, Maria said that she didn't want to have to wake them up several times. She would let them get themselves up using their alarm clock, and Maria wouldn't knock on their door until it was time for breakfast. If either of them was still in bed when she knocked, then they would both return to their previous bedtime for a week. If they were ready to eat and get to school on time, then they would continue to keep their new bedtime. The girls thought this was fair, and they agreed to help each other. This system worked well, and they only had to go back to their old bedtime for a week once. After that, Maria didn't have to worry about their sleeping habits. They were managing their own bedtimes.

Her fifth system helped establish structure and rules. Again, Maria knew this would be difficult for her. She hated to be a disciplinarian, especially now. Her darling girls were on the brink of becoming young ladies, and she didn't want to be the "mean mom." She decided to bring them in on the decision again and held a Family Meeting to discuss rules and schedules. Her girls weren't excited about having rules now that they were in middle school, but they brightened up at the idea that they could make up their own rules. In the end, their ideas for how their days should be structured and what rules they needed were surprisingly appropriate. Her girls were wise beyond their years, Maria decided. She could trust them. It was a good feeling.

Robert & Helen, Grandparenting While Autistic

"I just think she's moving too fast!" Robert paced around the kitchen table, chewing on his lip. "She needs to put the brakes on this whole engagement idea."

Parenting While Autistic

"Sit down, Robert, you're making me dizzy." Helen poured a cup of coffee and slid it over to him. "What do you have against Patrick, anyway? They've been dating for years. I thought you liked him."

"I'm not saying I don't like him. Patrick's a good guy. And he's good with Bobby, too."

"Exactly. Lena has never been happier. It's only natural that they would want to get married."

"But it's such a big change! And this is not a good time for Bobby. He's in middle school, for heaven's sake. That's a big enough change without having to move out of here and in with Patrick."

"I know you and Bobby both have trouble with change. I guess it's part of your autism."

"I guess so. But that doesn't mean it's not a valid point. Why rush into anything? There's plenty of time. They could wait until Bobby's out of middle school at least."

"And then you'd want them to wait until he's out of high school, and then out of college." Helen put her hand on his arm. "Face it, Robert, you're never going to be ready for them to move out on their own."

"This is not just about me wanting them here; it's about Bobby. Like I said, middle school is a hard time to make a major life change."

"But change happens all the time. Lots of middle school kids have to move, or their parents get divorced or remarried, and they survive."

"I know, but our Bobby's different. He takes things hard, especially unexpected changes."

5: Middle School

"This engagement is hardly unexpected. They've been a couple for five years and talking about getting engaged for two. They're very open with Bobby about it and have been all along. This is no shock for Bobby."

"Well, it is for me. I knew they'd leave home someday, but this is just too soon. I'm not ready."

"Well, dear, I hate to break it to you, but it doesn't matter if you're ready or not. Lena and Patrick are engaged, they will get married, and Lena and Bobby will move out. You and I don't have a say in it one way or the other."

"But what about Bobby? They'll be taking him away from the only home he's ever known, and from us! Kids his age don't adjust that quickly to a thing like that."

"Lena has been talking to Bobby's resource teacher, and she's keeping an eye on him to see if he seems anxious about anything. So far, he's been excited about the wedding and loves talking about moving in with Patrick."

"Hmph." Robert grunted and stared at his coffee cup. "I guess it doesn't matter what I think."

"The way I see it, you have two choices. You can keep on being a grouch about it and alienate your daughter and future son-in-law, and Bobby will certainly pick up on your negative attitude. Or you can get on board. If you can't find an ounce of happiness in your heart for Lena, then I suggest you fake it, and fake it good." Helen sounded firm. "I won't have your negative nonsense harming our relationship with our only child, so shape up."

"Okay, okay, I get it. No more grumpy old man."

"That's right. From now on, when they start talking about their wedding plans, I don't want to see your scowling face. Muster up a smile and say something nice."

"What if I can't think of anything nice to say? Communication is not my strong suit, you know."

"I know. Just choose between 'That sounds great!' and 'What a good idea!' and 'I can't wait!' You can't get in trouble with those mini-scripts. And don't forget to smile."

"What if I don't feel like smiling? I don't know how to make my face do things. It's just my face!"

"Tell one of your dad jokes. That always cracks you up."

"That reminds me—I just heard a new one from the geezers at the diner—"

"Better save it until Bobby gets home from school. You two have the same sense of humor."

"Yep, being autistic isn't the only thing we have in common."

And when Robert told him the joke later during his after-school snack, Bobby laughed until milk came out of his nose.

Daisy & Crow, Foster Parents

DAISY: *(stirs something in a mixing bowl)* Kitty, would you read me the next bit from the recipe?

KITTY: *(looks up from her game)* What? Where?

DAISY: It's right there. What ingredient comes next?

KITTY: *(looks at the open book)* Do you want me to bring it over and hold it up so you can read it?

DAISY: No, that's okay, just read me the third step on the instructions.

KITTY: Here, I'll bring it over. *(brings book and holds it up to Daisy)*

DAISY: You didn't have to come all the way over here. Just read me the part by the number three. I'm not supposed to stop stirring. If I stop stirring, I don't know what happens, but it's a bad thing, apparently.

KITTY: *(hesitantly)* It says … add. Add. That's number three, add.

DAISY: Add what? What's the next word?

KITTY: *(blows out air, peers at the page)* All. Add all.

DAISY: Really? I'm supposed to add all the rest of the ingredients at once? That doesn't seem right. Is there something after "Add all?"

KITTY: Yeah, there's more. It's some kind of milk. Moub milk. Do you have any moub milk?

DAISY: I've never heard of moub milk. Are you sure?

KITTY: It's right here, "Add all moub milk."

DAISY: *(hands her the bowl and spoon)* Here, you stir. Let me look at that recipe.

KITTY: *(stirs)* Yeah, you'd better read it yourself.

DAISY: It's almond milk. Add almond milk.

KITTY: Oh, yeah, I knew it. I mean, that was my next guess. Almond milk.

DAISY: It seems like you were substituting a 'u' for the 'n' and a 'b' for the 'd'.

Parenting While Autistic

KITTY: Well, you know, letters! They're pretty much inter-changeable, right? No big deal. *(stirs vigorously, looks down)*

DAISY: I don't think letters are interchangeable, actually. I think letters are letters. I mean, some of them have a blue or yellow or shiny feeling to them, but the letters always mean the same thing.

KITTY: Think about it, though. Look. Here's a spoon. *(holds up spoon vertically)* But now look at it. *(turns spoon upside down)* It's still a spoon. And look at it now. *(turns spoon to face right)* Spoon. And now. *(turns spoon to face left)* Spoon. It's always a spoon. It doesn't turn into a fork just because it's facing a different direction. That would be crazy.

DAISY: That would be crazy. But keep stirring.

KITTY: Oh, yeah. *(stirs)*

DAISY: You know I'm always up for a non sequitur or a trip down an unrelated rabbit hole, but I think you're trying to tell me something, and I want to understand. Why are we talking about spoons?

KITTY: We're not, we're talking about letters. You can't count on letters like you can spoons. They'll trick you.

DAISY: How do letters trick you?

KITTY: *(sighs)* When you hold it one way, it's a 'b', but when you turn it around, it's a 'd'. Upside down, it might be a 'p' or a 'q'.

DAISY: Is that why they say, "Mind your Ps and Qs"? I always wondered.

5: Middle School

KITTY: I never heard that one. But I do know that I can't trust letters. They mess with me every time.

DAISY: So it must be hard to read if you can't trust the letters.

KITTY: Yeah. Luckily, I'm an excellent fake reader.

DAISY: You're a fake reader?

KITTY: Sure. No one pays that much attention. I get by.

DAISY: Like masking.

KITTY: Masking?

DAISY: Yeah, it's an autistic thing. I used to try to do it a lot, fake being "normal," but it was exhausting. Luckily, I found D&D, and Crow. I don't have to mask or pretend to be someone else.

KITTY: Yeah, I guess it's kind of the same. There's usually a movie for the books we're supposed to read, so I know what's going on. Mostly in class I just avoid being called on. Since coming out as trans, I think they're embarrassed to call on me anyway, afraid they'll use the wrong name or pronoun. If the teacher does call on me during a discussion, I usually just agree with whoever said something just before me.

DAISY: So you've been faking reading all the way through school?

KITTY: Worked so far.

DAISY: And no one ever tried to help you learn how to read?

KITTY: Why would they? I'm an excellent faker.

DAISY: Oh, no, no, no, nope! This will not stand. You're starting high school next year! We need to get you some reading help, like, yesterday!

Parenting While Autistic

KITTY: I'd rather just keep on flying under the radar, if you don't mind. I get by. It's no big deal, really.

DAISY: That's a hard no. When Crow gets home, we'll have a Family Meeting. We're your foster parents now, and we will get you the help you need. Believe me, going through life faking is not a healthy long-term solution. I've been there.

KITTY: *(sighs)* Is this what it's like to have parents who actually notice you? Because you're kind of cramping my style.

DAISY: Welcome to Parenting, Daisy & Crow Style!

PARENT TO PARENT

"As our children got older, we noticed our eldest getting into disagreements with other children. He had ADHD, as I do, so we decided to put him in a different school with an emphasis on diversity. We thought this a perfect setting where they appreciated differences between individuals, rather than all being conformed to the same image that they thought was supposed to be. That was one of the smartest decisions my wife and I ever made. There was diversity and there was acceptance, and the fighting stopped.

"The kids would have their friends at our house, and I would make them things to eat and to drink and make sure that they were all safe. Our house was the magnet for all their friends to hang out. At this stage of their life, I was more of a background support, but I provided them a safe place to engage in their activities with their

5: Middle School

peers. They were all finding their places in the world. For the most part, it was their world, and I was happy they were finding it."

— James, late-diagnosed autistic dad

"To my own great surprise, I have found that being autistic has been a huge advantage in parenting in the middle school years. I know what it's like to feel different, out of place, and not quite understand what's going on in the social world around me. Added to that, when I'm dysregulated, I have trouble with mood swings and overwhelm, so I really know what it's like to feel like an adolescent! With my older daughters, I hadn't been diagnosed yet, but with my youngest daughter, I was diagnosed before she entered middle school. I've been so grateful for a better understanding of myself as I parent her through adolescence. As she's experiencing social, hormonal, and developmental changes which can overwhelm her, she's seen me get overwhelmed, which leads her to have greater empathy, compassion, and kindness, both towards others and towards herself. I think it's also been good for her to see me occasionally struggle, so she doesn't feel alone.

"We have a lot of conversations about which societal norms we embrace, such as diversity, empathy, and body positivity. We also talk about those norms that we don't embrace and why we don't, such as racism, judgmentalism, and body negativity. I think, in this area of my parenting, my autism is a gift. I've been assessing and analyzing social norms my entire life as I try to figure out the social world, and I'm accustomed to choosing some and rejecting others.

Parenting While Autistic

So, it's turned out to be a great advantage to have 'not fit in' my entire life, because it makes me much more intentional about where I want to work to fit in socially. My middle-school-aged daughter is learning this skill along with me, which means she is more immune to peer pressure."

— Krista, autistic mom

Chapter 6

High School

Contents Under Pressure

"Parents need to demonstrate a commitment to an orderly transfer of authority from themselves to their adolescent."

— Kenneth Wilgus

6: High School

igh school! Just when you thought it was safe to back off as a parent, it turns out they do still need you, maybe even more than ever. Don't get me wrong, you won't be involved at the same level of hands-on parenting that they needed in their early years, but it's too soon to stop parenting. Especially now that you're this close to the independence finish line.

High school students are particularly susceptible to peer pressure. As an autistic parent, you may or may not have felt that same pressure when you were their age. Many autistic teens can look at things logically and make their own decisions, such as whether it's smart to smoke, drink, or use drugs, regardless of what the other kids are doing. Other autistic teens may try so hard to make and keep friends that they will do things that they know are not a good idea just to be accepted. Typically, teens in the neuro-majority feel a much stronger pull toward their peers than they have in the past. They may crave advice and guidance from other high schoolers but ignore the same advice if it comes from their parents. It's not easy being the parent of a high schooler. You walk a tightrope between being a helicopter parent and an absent parent; don't lean too far in either direction and lose your balance.

DON'T BE A HELICOPTER PARENT

On the one hand, if you come on too strong and enforce strict rules that seem arbitrary to your teen, they may rebel and go too far in the opposite direction. Be aware of what most teens are doing, even though you do not base your decision on that information. If you're asking your high schooler to abide by rules which are significantly more stringent than their friends', be prepared to share your reasons behind the rules. Also, be prepared to listen to your child. They may be right when they say they're mature enough to be given greater freedom. You will gain their respect if you are willing to be flexible in response to their requests as long as they are within the boundaries of legality, morality, and safety.

DON'T BE AN ABSENT PARENT

On the other hand, while they may crave more freedom, this is not the time to completely check out as parents and allow them full control of their lives. They are on the road to being a legal adult and need to stretch their wings and figure things out, but don't take away their safety net. Be there if they want to talk, and just listen with respect and compassion and without judgment. Hold back on offering advice until they ask for it. After they've shared what they're thinking about, if they ask your opinion, consider asking them a question in response rather than just telling them what you think. You could ask, "Is it legal?" "Is it safe?" "Do you think it's a good idea?" "Do you feel good about it?" "If you do it, what might be the worst-case consequence, and how would you handle it if it came to that?" By giving them questions as they struggle to make a decision rather than giving them your opinion right away, it gives them the opportunity to reflect on their own personal values and come to a decision on their own. If you take a firm stand forbidding them to do something without listening to how they feel and think about it, the opportunity for them to learn how to make good decisions will be lost. You'll both feel better about the outcome if you've let them take the lead on the pro-and-con discussion.

SENSORY SMARTS

In high school, if your children are anything like the generations of teens before them, they will turn up the volume on their playlists. Your ears may be assaulted by loud music, not to mention laughter and high-pitched voices when their friends come over. To make it through these years with your eardrums intact, you'll need to remember the old reliable pair: Procedures and Protection.

Procedures for Sounds

Just as you created procedures to prevent some of the smells of the middle school years, you'll need to set some procedures for sound overload, too. Here are some of the sounds of the high school years, and procedures to handle them.

Music Volume

Finding the right volume for everyone in the family involves negotiation. Some people might be sensory seekers and want the volume turned up to 11. Others might be sensory avoiders, and for them 3 is the perfect volume. Get everybody in the family to share their preferences and try splitting the difference. Mark the volume dial at the agreed maximum volume, and make sure everyone understands that the knob is not to be turned above that mark. If there is no happy medium of volume that everyone can agree on, then the music listener can wear ear buds for listening (set at a safe, non-deafening level).

Voice Volume

If you have a child whose voice gets louder and louder the more excited they get, they may be unaware that their volume is painful to others. Let them help you come up with a nonverbal signal to let them know when this happens. If they choose the signal, they're less likely to be annoyed when you communicate that they're talking too loudly. Less likely, but chances are they will still be at least somewhat annoyed. That's life with a high schooler.

Sleepover Screams

When they get together with their friends, some kids use an extremely high pitch and loud volume to express their group approval and amusement. That is to say, when they laugh, they scream. If you're having a sleepover and one or both parents have super-sensitive hearing, you might want to set up a game or challenge for the slumber party. If you hear screams or squeals, since it is difficult to know if a scream signifies laughter or distress, you will come and interrupt the party to find out what is wrong. If an hour goes by and there is no need for you to check on them based on sound

6: High School

levels, consider rewarding them with a special treat, such as flavored popcorn instead of regular, or a plate of homemade brownies or cookies that they weren't expecting. You could arrange to leave the treat for them in the kitchen while you stay out of their way when their volume has been within acceptable limits. For high schoolers, the absence of parents is highly reinforcing.

Protections for Sounds

It's great to have procedures to prevent the sensory overload due to the volume preferred by many teenagers, but rules alone may not be enough. You'll want some protection from the auditory overload.

Competing Sounds

Try playing calming classical music or music of your choice to compete with sounds such as your child chewing, sniffing, or scratching.

Canceling Sounds

Use noise-canceling headphones or earplugs to make noises more tolerable.

High school students have always played their music at high volume, but with understanding, procedures, and protections, you can keep your sensory sanity.

MAKE FAMILY MEETINGS FUN

When your kids were in middle school, you started giving them more input into your Family Meetings. Now that they are in high school, consider transferring leadership of the meeting to them. They can choose the date and time, agenda, snacks, and post-meeting fun activity, within reason and with input. For example, if others in the family suggest a topic to bring up at the Family Meeting, they don't get to veto and ignore it just because they don't like it. Being a leader means listening to all sides on any issue, not just bulldozing their own agenda with no regard for anyone else's feelings. Of course, throughout their childhood, you will have been modeling this open and accepting leadership style yourselves. By handing over the reins of the Family Meetings when they are in high school, you are helping them on their path to adulting.

WEEKENDS THAT WORK

If you want your teenager to join the family for outings, it's a good idea to let them bring a friend. If your high school student has a boyfriend, girlfriend, or bestie, they'll have a better time if their friend is invited along. Of course, you probably won't invite a friend to every family weekend event, but doing so occasionally when it seems like something they would enjoy is a good way to show your high schooler that you recognize that they have a life outside of your immediate family. It's part of growing up. Also, you never

6: High School

know which high school romance may become your future son- or daughter-in-law. Being welcoming and accepting of their friends and sweethearts will lead to continuing strong family relationships after they leave the nest.

FICTIONAL FAMILIES

Trish & Bill, Autistic Parents

"Did you go with Jim to rent his tux for the prom?" Trish repetitively twisted the dish towel in her hands.

"He didn't want me to." Bill recognized that Trish was feeling anxious by how tightly the towel in her hands was twisted. "It's okay, though. I gave him my credit card, and he went in alone."

"Alone? Do you think he knew how to do it?"

"He seemed to. He came back happy." Bill and Trish were both aware that their non-autistic son was having a very different high school experience than they themselves had.

"Did you rent your tux yourself when you went to prom?"

Bill chuckled. "No way! My mom called my date's mom and asked her what color her daughter would be wearing. Then she rented me a tux to match and helped me pick out a corsage."

"You were lucky to have her." Trish noticed the dish towel in her hands, untwisted it, and set it down. "How did you ask her to prom?"

"I didn't." Bill looked down. "My mother's best friend's daughter didn't have a date, and we were both shy, so they thought we'd be a perfect match."

"And were you?"

"What do you think?" Bill smiled. "Until I met you, I never had a date that wasn't awkward and painful to remember. How about you? Did you enjoy your prom?"

"I didn't go. Did I miss much?"

"That depends," Bill said. "Do you enjoy loud music, crowds of perfumed people, shiny spinning mirror balls hanging from the ceiling, and all of it jammed into an echo chamber of a gymnasium?"

Trish shuddered. "It sounds awful! How will Jim bear it?"

"You know, he's not like us. He seems to actually enjoy the noise, lights, and crowds at the pizza arcade."

The two sat in silence for a moment, lost in thought. Finally, Trish broke the silence.

"He's going to be okay, isn't he?"

Bill pulled her into a bear hug. "He's going to be better than okay."

Justin & Maggie, Autistic Dad Adoption Story

"Justin, take a look at this." Maggie turned her computer toward him to show him their local paper's website. "There's an article about Ray in here. I mean, it doesn't mention his name, but I'm sure it's him."

"Seriously?" Justin sat beside her. "What is it?"

"It seems to be good news, but it gives me a creepy feeling. You read it and tell me what you think."

6: High School

Justin read the article. It was about the high school football team taking turns sitting with a special student at lunch and how one of the cheerleaders planned to go to a dance with him. The kids were being hailed as heroes, with lots of smiling pictures, and one candid shot showing a football player sitting in the cafeteria across from Ray. Ray's back was to the camera, which is probably how they got away with printing it without permission.

"This is inspo porn." Justin leaned back with a disgusted look on his face.

"Porn?" Maggie quickly turned the computer back to look at the pictures again.

"Inspo porn is when people in the neuro-majority write about helping disabled people. The idea is to show how wonderful they are for what is basically just human kindness. I guess the idea of being kind to a disabled person without getting media attention is too much to ask."

"I never even heard of this." Maggie looked thoughtful.

"Have you ever read a story about an autistic kid who could shoot baskets, or a blind or deaf valedictorian, or a young man with intellectual disability getting a job greeting people in a big box store? Everybody makes a big deal about how inspiring they are, but they're just doing normal things. It's not brave to live your life in a wheelchair; it's just living your life. But typical people get all misty-eyed when they read articles about 'poor disabled kids' just being themselves."

Parenting While Autistic

"I had no idea!" Maggie turned pink, remembering the times she'd had the same reaction. "But why do they do it?"

"The kids in this article are probably going to put it on their college applications and expect that their 'compassion' will help them get into the school of their choice. Maybe they're sharing it with their followers for clout. It's not real friendship, it's just for show."

"Are you sure? Ray is such a likable guy, maybe they really want to be friends with him."

"If that were true, the football team wouldn't 'take turns' sitting with him at lunch. And the cheerleader wouldn't have alerted the media that she was thinking about going to a dance with a 'special kid.' They may not even realize how gross this is, because they never thought about it from Ray's perspective."

"What should we do?" Maggie looked back at the article with a cold feeling in her stomach.

"Well, Ray seems pretty happy when he comes home from school, so I think he's fine. But I do want to schedule a meeting with his case manager to talk about this. We never gave permission for him to be in this article, and even though they didn't mention his name or show his face, he's pretty identifiable."

"What about that girl who said she'd go to a dance with him? If she really likes him, I don't want to stop him from going to a dance, but I don't him taken advantage of or hurt, either."

"Let's ask his case manager if this girl or any girls in his class seem to really like him in a romantic way. And if this cheerleader

6: High School

has never spent any time getting to know him as a person, we can ask the school to talk to her about the article. They should tell her not to ask him to the dance if she's doing it out of pity or to get social media likes. If she really wanted to date him, she would spend a lot more time with him at school when there are no cameras on her. She could text him, have conversations with him, whatever kids do when they like each other, and not just jump right into going to a dance."

"That's a good idea. I'll call his case manager and set up a meeting."

"Thanks. And I'll have a talk with Ray when he comes home from school, you know, beyond the usual 'How was school?' I'll ask him about his friends and who he likes to hang out with. Maybe find out if he really enjoys the football players eating with him or if he thinks it's weird."

"That's right. We need to know how he feels about all this before we meet with the school." Maggie put her hand on Justin's. "Thank you for telling me about this. I honestly never heard of inspo porn before. I just want Ray to be happy, however that looks for him."

"I think he is happy, but I think we're right to look into this. He may be a teenager, but he still needs our protection sometimes."

Parenting While Autistic

Lucia & Naima, Two Autistic Moms

"So, what do you think about Noah?" Lucia loaded the dishwasher with Naima rinsing the dishes.

"Noah? He's a good kid." Naima handed her a plate. "Why do you ask?"

"Well, it just seems like Ruby's spending a lot of time with him, that's all."

"Don't you like Noah?"

"That's not it, Noah's great. Really." Lucia put the plate in the dishwasher. "But do they have to spend that much time together? He's over here nearly every day after school."

"Of course he is; he's Ruby's boyfriend. They're going to spend time together."

"Boyfriend?" Lucia stopped and turned to look at her wife. "I thought they were just friends. He's her boyfriend?"

"Yeah. I guess you didn't pick up on the clues? How they act together?"

"I'm not good at the subtle cues. Anyway, I always kind of thought that Ruby and Samantha would get together."

"They're best friends, but they're both hetero. They'll never date."

"Are you saying Ruby is heterosexual?"

"We always knew this was a possibility. Come on, let's sit down and talk."

"I just don't want her to get hurt. Men can be so cruel."

"Women can be mean, too." Naima bumped her shoulder against Lucia's. "I mean, have you ever met a fifth-grade girl? Brutal!"

6: High School

"You know what I mean."

"I know. You've been hurt by men, and you worry about Ruby. But Noah is not like the men who hurt you. He's a good kid."

"I know."

"And Ruby's smart. Do you think she'd let some jerk take advantage of her?"

"I did at her age."

"Me, too. But now we're raising a daughter to value her own worth. Ruby will never sell herself short. She will never accept being disrespected." Naima took Lucia's hand. "You do know this, right?"

Lucia sighed. "Yeah, I know. I just thought Ruby and Samantha made a cute couple."

"They are adorable BFFs. Ruby will have all the friends she wants, and boyfriends or girlfriends. She knows we'll accept her no matter what and that we've got her back." Naima gave Lucia a stern look. "But that means accepting her as who she is, even if her sexuality is different from ours."

"You're right, of course. I wouldn't want her to go through what I did when I told my family that I'm a lesbian. I thought my father would disown me."

"Your family came around eventually, and so did mine, but with Ruby, we can skip the closet trauma and the coming-out drama."

Lucia smiled. "I guess she's pretty lucky to have us as her moms, isn't she?"

"I know that's right. Her generation really believes that love is love is love, and she won't have to be ashamed of her choices."

"Thank goodness!"

Naima grinned at her wife. "Another reason to be welcoming and accepting of Ruby's boyfriend is that he might end up being the father of our future grandchildren."

Lucia gasped. "What? They're not—!"

"No, they're not pregnant, as far as I know. I just want to look ahead to the future. We should treat every boyfriend with kindness in case they end up part of our family forever."

"Then maybe we should invite Noah to come along on our weekend hike?"

"If Ruby hasn't already asked him, then yeah, let's tell her that he's always welcome to join us."

By being open and accepting of their daughter's different choices and by treating her relationship with respect rather than thinking of it as a "crush" or "puppy love," Lucia and Naima laid the groundwork for a wonderful relationship with their future son-in-law, whoever he might turn out to be.

Maria & Santiago, Undiagnosed Autistic Mom

Maria paced and wrung her hands repeatedly. She didn't know what to do. It was almost Easter, and there were no eggs decorated. None. Not one. This had never happened before, and she felt a tightness in her chest thinking about it.

When her girls were little, every year they decorated Easter eggs together during spring break. Maria would prepare the hot water and vinegar baths and let each girl drop drips of food coloring into

6: High School

the cups. Then they used the little wire holders to lower the eggs into the cups, deciding whether to let them stay and darken in the cup or pull them out quickly for a pastel shade. Even though she hated the smell of the vinegar, the ritual was important to Maria.

In middle school, the girls had been less interested. They'd each made one egg and then run off to chat with their friends online. Maria had dyed the remaining eggs herself, and she did not enjoy it. But it had to be done, didn't it? It was a tradition.

Now that Faith and Hope were in high school, though, they let her know in no uncertain terms that they would not be dyeing eggs this year. They wanted to have their friends over after Mass, eat candy, and just have fun on their own, without decorating any eggs with their mother.

Maria paced a bit faster as she tried to figure out a way through this. Changing a long-standing tradition like this was painful to even consider, but she couldn't force her daughters to dye eggs if they didn't want to.

Or could she?

What if she said that if they didn't dye Easter eggs with her there would be no candy? Or their friends couldn't come over? Or that they'd be grounded? That would bring them around, wouldn't it?

No, she realized that even if they agreed to dye eggs to avoid punishment, she couldn't make them enjoy it. She'd just have to give up a tradition that had been important to her but was no longer important to her daughters.

Parenting While Autistic

Maria sank into a chair and put her hands over her face. Blocking out all light helped her focus when she was distraught. She tried to imagine a new, different Easter tradition, something that everyone could enjoy. When she got her idea, she took down her hands and turned her face up toward the light. This was the right solution.

On Easter Sunday, when they came home from Mass and the girls brought their friends, the young people gathered around the table, chatting and snacking on chocolate rabbit ears. Maria came in and placed a crystal bowl that had been her mother's in the center of the table. The bowl was filled with pure, white, hard-boiled eggs. Then she left and came back with two glasses, each filled with a bouquet of fine-tipped markers, in all the colors of the rainbow. She put one glass down on each side of the bowl and then stepped back.

"What are we supposed to do with these?" one of the girls asked.

"Nothing. You're not supposed to do anything with them. But you may decorate them if you feel like it."

"What if we don't feel like it?"

"I think a bowl of white eggs is lovely as it is. But if anyone wants to add color, you may." Then Maria went back into the living room and sat down. She heard the girls continuing to chat and giggle together, and then heard them talking about what colors and designs they were using. They were doing it! They were decorating eggs! Maria's heart filled with joy at the thought. She didn't need to be in the room; she didn't need to be part of it. Actually, she preferred enjoying social occasions at a distance. But she knew that she had made this happen. Their laughter and enjoyment were because she had let go of an old tradition and created a new one.

It felt delightful.

Robert & Helen, Grandparenting While Autistic

"I'll bet you can't guess what my favorite part of Lena's wedding is going to be," Robert smiled, waiting for Helen to make the wrong guess.

"Well, it can't be the ceremony, or wearing a suit and tie. And it can't be the reception, with all those people, and being expected to stand up and give a toast."

"You got that right!" Robert chuckled at how well his wife knew him. Since being diagnosed with autism, same as Bobby, they had both been learning more about what made him tick.

"It must be the honeymoon."

"What?" Robert looked at her in surprise. "It's not our honeymoon, it's Lena's and Patrick's! What made you guess that?"

"Because Bobby will be here with us for the two weeks they're in Coronado."

Robert shook his head but couldn't keep from smiling. "I thought I had you on that one, but you guessed it. It'll be great to have him here, just the three of us, before he moves away for good."

"It's not like he'll be across the world, only in the next town over. He can come over whenever he likes."

Parenting While Autistic

"Yeah, but high schoolers don't like hanging out with old geezers. We'll probably never see him again until it's time to go to his wedding someday."

"Nonsense. You're just feeling sorry for yourself. Why don't you do something useful instead?"

"Hmph. Like organizing the garage?"

"Don't act like that's a chore; you love organizing all your bits and bobs. But I was thinking you should plan something special for you and Bobby to do while his mom is on her honeymoon."

"Like what?"

"Well, what's Bobby interested in? Think of something he'd like, then run it past his mom to make sure she approves."

"Like I'd suggest anything she wouldn't approve of," Robert grumbled.

"She is still his mother, and until he's eighteen she has parental rights, so don't go off on some wild trip without her consent."

"I'll also need Bobby's okay, you know. He's not a little kid anymore. I can't just assume he's going to like whatever I want to do."

"That's true. So what do you think he'd like?"

"Well, he's always watching those Japanese cartoon whatchama-callits."

"Anime, I think you mean. He loves it. What can you think of that has to do with anime, though?"

6: High School

"He happened to mention that there's a convention in town during the time his mom will be gone, and I figured I'd take him to that. He can teach me a thing or two about that stuff."

"Anime. You might want to start by learning the name of it. Just saying." Helen smiled at him so he knew she wasn't really scolding him.

"Yeah, I know. So I guess I'd better run it by Bobby and Lena before I buy the tickets."

"Definitely ask Lena first, and then after she says okay, you can ask Bobby if he'd like to go."

Robert got Lena's blessing, and when he brought it up to Bobby, the boy was thrilled. The two of them had a great time at the convention. Since they were both autistic, they understood when either of them needed a break from all the sensory and social overload, and they took it at their own pace.

After Lena came back from her honeymoon and Bobby went home, Robert and Helen missed him, but they maintained a close relationship. Bobby knew the door was always open for him at their home. If it was hard for him to get used to living with a stepdad, he could always spend a weekend with his grandparents. Just knowing that was a great stress reducer for this autistic teen.

Parenting While Autistic

Daisy & Crow, Foster Parents

DAISY: What do you mean, they won't sign your IEP? I thought parents had to sign it.

KITTY: They're supposed to sign it so I can get reading help in school, but they just won't sign.

CROW: Why not?

KITTY: *(hesitating, head down)* It's my name.

DAISY: What about your name? I don't understand.

KITTY: Well, now that I'm in high school, the school psych did some more testing to show that I still need help. She put "Kevin" on the front page to match my legal name from my birth certificate, but then she refers to me as "Kitty" on all the other pages.

DAISY: Of course. That's your name.

KITTY: But it's not the name my parents gave me. They're being total transphobes and jerks about it, and I'm afraid I'll lose the help I'm getting at school. Can't you sign it for me? You're more parents to me than they are.

DAISY: I'll sign anything if it will help.

CROW: Except that we can't.

DAISY: I'm pretty sure I can forge their signatures.

CROW: But as a lawful good, you won't do it.

DAISY: *(shakes fist)* Curse my lawfulness! Wait, you're chaotic neutral, you can forge them!

CROW: I can forge steel, but I will never forge a signature. If we get in legal trouble, we could lose Kitty.

6: High School

KITTY: I don't want you to get in trouble. I just don't know what to do.

CROW: You know we'll do whatever we can for you, but we don't have educational rights, just foster rights. Your parents haven't lost their educational rights. We're thrilled that you can live here, but we can't sign any official school papers.

DAISY: What about Sandra Markowitz?

KITTY: The social worker?

DAISY: Maybe she can sign.

CROW: I don't know, but I'll call her. We will take care of this one way or the other, Kitty, I'm sure of it.

DAISY: We are behind you, 1000 percent!

KITTY: I only need 100, but thanks, guys. You are the best!

Crow did call Sandra Markowitz, and she took on the educational system, unwilling to let Kitty fall through the cracks. Eventually the school psychologist amended the report to show Kitty's legal deadname for compliance with the law and Kitty's parents but gave the copy with her true name to Kitty. Sandra had a long talk with Kitty's mother and made arrangements for the key IEP team members to meet with her after her work day was over to go over the paperwork. Even though Kitty's dad still refused to sign anything, saying that his son was dead to him, it was enough for her mother to sign the IEP. Kitty continued receiving the special help she needed throughout her high school years. By the time she graduated, she could read at the fifth-grade level, and as soon as she turned eighteen, she legally changed her name to Kitty. High school wasn't easy for her, but having foster parents like Daisy and Crow and a social worker who cared made all the difference.

PARENT TO PARENT

"I taught my children to be independent from a very early age. My daughter still reminds me of when she was five years old and she asked me a question about the store and I told her to go ask the cashier. She thought I was crazy for expecting her to do that, but she did go ask and get her answer. When she was in high school, she was always the leader. She credits her leadership qualities to my insistence on independence at an early age. I wanted them to each find their own ground, so they were allowed the freedom to explore their world in their eyes and not just mine.

"The teen years were the hardest, when kids are supposed to begin finding themselves and exploring their worlds and relationships. I was never very good at change, so that was very difficult for me."

— James, late-diagnosed autistic dad

"Being autistic, my own high school years were challenging, most especially because I don't have a sad affect, so anytime I was sad, disappointed, or fearful, most people around me just thought I was

6: High School

angry. At the time, this was very painful, but as a parent, I am deeply grateful for that experience because I know firsthand what it's like to be misunderstood and not be able to express your emotions well enough to clear up the misunderstanding.

"In addition to this, I feel quite comfortable refusing to play by society's 'rules,' so when all the parents around me kept sighing and telling me the teenage years were going to be horrible, I set out to figure out how to have really positive high school years with my older daughters. Personally, I found the late middle school years the most challenging period of raising adolescents. By the time my daughters were in high school, they were fabulous people to be around and I thoroughly enjoyed those years. In this, I think part of what helped was that I'm not sentimental, so I wasn't worried about them leaving the nest, and their very necessary individuation didn't frighten me. Quite the reverse! I was excited to watch my girls grow up and see what directions they wanted to take as they embarked on their adult lives.

"I also believed very strongly that children need skills, so I gave my daughters a lot of opportunities to build life skills—basic household skills like laundry and cooking so they could take care of themselves, learning to host social events so they could facilitate community, learning to manage money so they could be independent. I saw the whole goal of their teenage years to be a training ground for their eventual independence, and since this coincided with their neurological development, it was a really positive time. I did a lot of reading about the adolescent brain, and it was very helpful to have information that showed me what was going on in their brains and what they needed.

"At every point in my daughters' teenage years, I tried to express to them in both verbal and nonverbal ways how important they were to me and how I was trying to support them in their journey towards independence. I certainly wasn't a perfect parent, but I think my kids knew I was trying, and that really sustained our relationship. I also made it clear to them that they could come and talk to my husband and me about anything and that we meant it—we would commit to always listening to them without judging them. I didn't always understand their struggles (for example, my second daughter was very social and I had trouble meeting her needs because of my own introversion), but I tried to show them that I was always willing to make whatever effort was needed on their behalf. I think this goes a long way towards raising adolescents—you want to give them space, but you want them to know you've always got their back."

— Krista, autistic mom

Chapter 7

Parenting Adults

Finding Your New Normal

"Parents can only give good advice or put them on the right paths, but the final forming of a person's character lies in their own hands."

— Anne Frank

"Our job as parents is to teach our kids not to need us. And it hurts, but when you see them as accomplished, confident, kind, thoughtful, responsible people, then you know you've done your job."

— Barack Obama

7: Parenting Adults

Finally, the parenting journey is coming to an end, or rather, to a crossroads. You will always be their parents and they will always be your children, long after they have passed their eighteenth birthday, or their twenty-first, or their sixtieth. Parenting is forever, but the responsibility for directing and teaching our children is limited. Once they are legal adults, we are no longer liable for their actions, and it is not our job to tell them how to live their life. It's hard for every parent to make that transition, but autistic parents may find it even more challenging. If you have a strong preference for continuing in one direction rather than transitioning from one thing to another, you may have more trouble than others in letting go. After years of making and monitoring rules for your children, that is no longer your job. As adults, they should decide things for themselves, such as how late they stay up, where they go and with whom, and what they eat if they buy and prepare their own food.

RULES

But wait (I hear you cry), if they're under my roof, don't they have to live by my rules?

Yes, you can continue to require them to abide by your parental authority while they're living under your roof, but think about the potential outcomes. If you enforce arbitrary or overly strict rules on your adult kids and hold them hostage just because it's your house, be prepared for the consequences. Many young people move out of their parents' homes for this very reason. They may be able to afford their own apartment or live with others, which is a natural progression of adulting, and that's great.

However, it's better if their exit into the world is a happy, natural one, when they're ready, not after a slammed door and an angry "Oh, yeah? Then I won't live under your roof!" If they leave in anger, it will be hard for them to come back later if they find out they aren't ready to make it on their own yet. Young people have become couch-surfers or homeless because they left on an angry note after they felt their parents had smothered and infantilized them with childish rules, and they didn't know how to go back.

Which rules are appropriate to maintain, and which ones should be left behind when your child turns eighteen? That's a good question, and the answer is different for every family.

RULES OF MORALITY

If you have strong religious or moral beliefs that you hold dear, then it's certainly within your rights to make household rules that reflect these beliefs. If you are morally opposed to pre-marital sexual activity, you may make a rule that your child may not have a romantic partner spend the night in their room under your roof. If you are opposed to guns, you may make a rule that none will be allowed under your roof. Just remember, what they do as adults outside of your home is no longer your business. They may make different choices than you, and that's okay.

7: Parenting Adults

RULES OF LEGALITY

You have every right to enforce the laws of your state and region within your household, and you should. You may declare your home to be a drug-free zone. If your county has a legal limit on how many pets may live in a single household, you may forbid your adult child to bring in additional pets. It's smart to maintain a household that upholds the law.

RULES OF PROPERTY

You have the right to expect that your property and belongings will be respected. In the past, if your child had broken a vase, you may have simply replaced it yourself. Part of living with children is understanding that things get broken. Now that your child is an adult, if they break something that you purchased, or harm your house or property, it is within your rights to ask them to pay for the damages. Of course, if the damage was accidental, then as a loving parent you may choose to be gracious and let it go. On the other hand, if they had a party in your home while you were away, it got out of hand, and your rugs or furniture were ruined, it is only right that they should pay to have things put back to rights. If they can't afford it all at once, consider a reasonable payment plan that is not overly punitive but which you will both agree to. Get it in writing, which you both sign. Being an adult means they take responsibility for their actions.

RULES OF RESPONSIBILITY

On that note, an adult child living with you should take on their share of adult responsibilities for general housekeeping and maintenance. They may be accustomed to having a parent pack their lunch, prepare their meals, and do all of the cleaning and housework, but as an adult, things should change. If your adult child is still living with you, write up at a Family Meeting a list of all of the tasks that must be done to keep the household running smoothly, and divide them up between all adults in the home. If your child says that they can't do that because they have a job, remind them that most adults have jobs and homes that they must care for. It's time for them to step up and do their fair share.

CONTINUING EDUCATION

After high school, your child may go on to attend the college you had dreamed of for them, or a community college, or trade school, or they may take a "gap year" before starting college. They may opt out of continuing education altogether because they've had enough of school, or because they don't want to be burdened by student loan debt, or because their chosen career doesn't require a degree. Whatever they choose, the direction of their education is no longer your decision to make. Support them in making their own life decisions without judging them. They are becoming adults in a different world than the one you came of age in. Trust that they will find their way and be happy in it.

7: Parenting Adults

ENTERING THE WORKFORCE

Dr. Martin Luther King, Jr., said, "All labor that uplifts humanity has dignity and importance and should be undertaken with painstaking excellence." Remember these words when your child chooses their career path. They may not make the choices you would have made for them, but their choices are valid. No one's worth is dependent on their bank account, and your child's work may be different from what you expected of them but no less valuable.

LEAVING THE NEST

Many young adults in this generation find it difficult or impossible to move out and maintain their own home. Despite tough times economically, many young people are able to move out and establish their own households. Whether it's a tiny studio apartment, a shared house with friends, a condominium, tract home, or a mini-mansion, they have finally found their wings and flown away, leaving you in an empty nest. There are parents who mourn this natural occurrence and parents who rejoice in it. Most parents experience both the joy of their rediscovered freedom and the sorrow that can come with change and missing your kids. This is all normal, whatever your neuro-type. There are a lot of feelings around empty nesting, but you can make it a positive place in your life.

If you live with a partner, this is a time you can go back to the kinds of things you used to do before you had children, such as spontaneous date nights and weekend adventures. If you live alone, enjoy the opportunity to be the only one to decide what to watch or listen to. You are the one ruler of the remote.

When it comes to your newly independent children, two things to pay attention to during this time are boundaries and a welcome mat.

EMPTY NEST BOUNDARIES

You may need to set up boundaries for yourself once your adult children leave home. If they grew up there, they probably still view it as their own home and may come and go as they please without advance notice. Maybe they need to do laundry, or they want a home-cooked meal, or they don't have air conditioning. Maybe they just miss your company. For whatever reason, they are likely to feel comfortable dropping in unannounced at their convenience.

Many autistic parents strongly dislike surprises, so unexpected guests, even the children you adore, can be a source of anxiety. You have the right to tell your children that they need to text you in advance of any visit. It's not that they're not welcome; it's just that you need to know what to expect on any given day, so drop-ins should be discouraged.

You have the right to set the boundaries that are comfortable for you and to enforce them. If someone tries to overstep the limits you have set and comes over without advance warning, you have the right to kindly and lovingly tell them that this is not a good time for a visit. Then arrange a time for them to come over another day, and put it on the calendar. It's best if you set up your boundaries in advance and make sure they are aware that they will not be invited inside if they just show up. It may feel cruel, but it's not; it's a matter of respect and self-advocacy. If they do show up unannounced, do not let them inside, not even "just for a minute." If you do, the message communicated is that your boundaries don't apply to them. Turn them away with love and a promise of a visit soon, and thank them for understanding how important your boundaries are.

EMPTY NEST WELCOME MAT

Of course, you will want to have the welcome mat out for scheduled visits with your grown kids. Some families have a regular time each week, such as Sunday supper, when the kids have a standing invitation to come by for a meal and conversation. It's good to let them know that this is not mandatory but rather an open door for them when their schedule allows. It can be helpful if they let you know in advance whether they'll be there on any particular Sunday (or whatever day you choose) so you can plan the meal accordingly and know what to expect.

Other families prefer a monthly extended family outing, such as a picnic with all the grown kids and grandkids. Choose a familiar, safe place for the youngest generation to play while you and your kids catch up, whether at a park, or in your own backyard.

When families live farther away, you may gather together seasonally (e.g., with an annual summer gathering) or during special holidays. You can always keep in touch by phone or video chat between visits.

The important thing to remember is that you can and should respect your own boundaries against surprise drop-ins while also laying out the welcome mat for planned gatherings.

NEW SENSORY SMARTS

Now that you have an empty nest, you can reclaim your sensory environment. Do you love listening to opera or the Beatles, but your kids hated it? Now you can fill your home with your favorite music, or none at all. You can finally get rid of the unwashed gym sock and stale pizza smells emanating from your adult child's room and replace it with scents you love, whether it's eucalyptus, lavender, sage, or anything that pleases you. Allow yourself a sensory makeover for your newly empty nest. It will help you move into the empty nest stage of your life with the balance that comes with re-creating your own sensory world. Naturally, if you live with a partner, this should be a joint venture, designing a sensory environment that the two of you can enjoy together.

7: Parenting Adults

OLD FAMILY MEETINGS

Just because you no longer have children living under your roof doesn't mean you should abandon Family Meetings. It's time to return to the old Family Meetings for two if you live with a partner. Schedule time to compare calendars, discuss needed tasks around the house, and plan for all the things you want to do together now that it's just the two of you again. This is a time in life when many couples grow closer than ever, and Family Meetings and Date Nights are part of making the most of it.

WEEKENDS ARE YOURS AGAIN

This is your opportunity to reclaim your time. As empty nesters, your weekends are yours again. Do the things you love to do without worrying about whether your kids will enjoy them. It's also important to plan family gatherings with your kids, and eventually perhaps their kids, to keep the family bonds strong. So that everyone knows what to expect, consider planning a regular time for an all-family vacation, holiday celebration, or weekend day trip, or just inviting them to visit you at your home. If everyone can agree to get together on the second Saturday of the month, you will have a plan to look forward to and the security of knowing you don't have to start from scratch to figure out when everybody can get together. If one of your kids can't make it, do what you can as far as self-management and coping skills to adjust to the unexpected change without assigning blame or guilt. Enjoy the times you have with them, and when you're apart, enjoy your time alone or with your partner.

FICTIONAL FAMILY UPDATES

Trish & Bill, Autistic Parents, Empty Nest Update

James, Trish and Bill's only son, decided not to go to his mom's college that she loved and still worked for, or to his dad's alma mater. Instead, he followed his heart and went to culinary school. He got a job working in a restaurant, and in his early twenties he moved out and rented a home with several other young people he'd met in the food industry. James was happy in his life. He didn't need the fame or fortune of being the top chef in a Michelin-starred restaurant, but he did occasionally dream of competing on a television cooking show.

The house seemed empty after James moved out, and both Trish and Bill found it difficult to adjust to such a big change in their lives. However, they had each other. After several months of feeling vaguely out of balance and in a fog, they decided they would need to be purposeful about creating their new life as a couple again instead of as parents. They reinstated Family Meetings and used them to plan fun Date Nights and excursions related to their own special interests, not their child's activities. They fell in love with each other all over again, not that they'd ever fallen out of love. Trish and Bill found renewal in their post-parenting relationship.

Some years later, when they retired, there was another period of difficult adjustment where they felt out of harmony and disjointed. Again, they needed to make a retirement plan for how they would spend their days, balancing time together with time apart, which suited them. Later, when James got married and started his own family, they loved having them over and spoiling their grandchildren. It was always a great relief when they all went home, though. Bill and Trish weren't used to the level of social and sensory input and excitement that went on whenever the grands came over. Fortunately, James and his wife understood their autism, and they didn't get offended if Trish or Bill had to retreat to a place of quiet and solitude in the middle of a visit. Their lives took on a predictable and enjoyable pattern, which worked beautifully for them.

Justin & Maggie, Autistic Dad Adoption Story, Soon-to-be-Empty Nest Update

Justin and Maggie's boy, Ray, was able to stay in high school receiving an individualized, specialized education until he was twenty-two, at which time he felt ready to move on. He wanted to be as independent as possible, so his parents signed him up for training at the vocational rehabilitation center in their city. One option was a work center where disabled adults could work with others like them, but the pay was shockingly low, and Ray didn't seem particularly interested in what they were doing when he visited. Then they checked out an arts program, where disabled adults participated in art, drama, and music. Ray thought it looked like fun, but at twenty-two, he wanted a real job. They were referred to a coffee shop, operated by the same program, that trained and employed disabled people to work as dishwashers, bussers, waiters, cashiers, sandwich-makers, and even baristas. Ray loved it, and they signed him up for the program that same day. After a brief waiting period, he started his training.

Ray loved working at the café. He continued to live at home with his parents, and they weren't in a hurry to help him find other living arrangements. Justin and Maggie knew that they wouldn't live forever and that they needed to think about the future for Ray, but it was hard. Group homes sounded institutional to them, so they didn't visit any or get to know what was available. That would be a problem for tomorrow.

Then Ray met Sydney. Sydney was a young woman with Down syndrome, a couple of years older than Ray, who worked with him at the café. It was love at first sight for Ray and Sydney. They shared so many interests, and their senses of humor meshed so that they often dissolved into giggles over a text or picture the other had sent. After dating for a year, Ray proposed, and the young couple asked their parents' blessings.

It was a bit terrifying for Justin and Maggie to think about their special little guy being a husband and maybe a father one day. Could he do it? Would his disability stop him from living the full life they'd always hoped for him? What if the marriage failed?

7: Parenting Adults

What if the young couple needed more support than they could offer one another? After all, they were both intellectually impaired. Was it smart for them to get married?

It didn't matter if it was a smart idea or not. This was a decision made by Ray and Sydney based on love, mutual support, and a strong desire to make their marriage work. No amount of discussion by their parents would dissuade them from their plan. Justin and Maggie had many late-night discussions as they lay awake, worrying about their son, but eventually they realized that they were being ableist. Why shouldn't two people in love get married? People did it all the time. They scheduled a dinner with the young couple and Sydney's parents, and gave their blessing and pledge to help support them and their marriage in any way they could. It turned out Ray and Sydney had already researched their future. There was a group home not far from the café which was willing to provide a minimally supported housing opportunity for a married couple with developmental disabilities. It was a fairly new concept but an important one to support, and they were excited to be the first couple in the group home.

Ray and Sydney chose to be child-free and devoted themselves to their two tuxedo cats, Sir and Ma'am. They were grateful for their parents' support and for the chance to live their own lives as adults without discrimination based on their disability. With their families' full support, they planned their dream wedding.

Justin and Maggie started preparing for their upcoming status change to empty nesters. They weren't quite ready to take any long trips on their own because they still wanted to be nearby in case Ray needed them, but they planned several weekend trips for two. They also noticed that at some point during their child-raising years their Date Nights had fallen off the calendar, so now they made sure to put it back on as a weekly routine. Justin knew that getting used to any change was hard for him, but he didn't want his own need for the familiar to stand in the way of his son's readiness to leave the nest. He kept his concerns to himself or shared them only with Maggie, publicly maintaining optimistic support for Ray and Sydney. It was a bit like the masking he used to do before he and Maggie knew about his autism, but this time it felt like the right thing to do and not like a burden. The more he wore his optimistic mask around the kids, the more he felt his inner optimism grow.

The kids were going to be okay.

Lucia & Naima, Two Autistic Moms, Empty Nest Update

When Ruby moved in with her boyfriend, Noah, Lucia and Naima were delighted to be free from the smells and fumes emanating from Ruby's room when she worked on her art projects. No more headaches and wearing face masks indoors! They liked Noah, even though he was a boy, which was still hard for them to wrap their minds around.

Then Ruby told them she planned to travel and do more art rather than go to college. This was hard for them to accept. They'd each been the first college graduates in their families, and education

7: Parenting Adults

was important to them. Since before Ruby was even born, they had dreamed of her future path from childhood to adulthood, and the journey had always included her graduating from a four-year university. How was she ever going to make a living and be independent without a BA?

They called an emergency Family Meeting and sat her down to warn her about the mistake she was making. They painted a picture of the life of poverty as a starving artist that would surely be hers without a college diploma. Ruby giggled with the same little smile that her moms had often shared when she had done something cute as a child. She thought they were adorable for worrying about that but told them their fears were groundless. Turns out she was already doing great without a degree. In all the time she had spent in her room working on her art, she had been creating YouTube videos and paid courses, demonstrating how to craft jewel-like resin bracelets and pendants, and tiny but incredibly realistic clay food, some of which she sold. Corporate sponsors sent her free art materials to showcase on her channel, and she got a percentage of profits every time one of her viewers purchased their products from her link, which was frequent. She had patrons who sent her money every month, and she thanked them by making up little songs with their names during her closing credits at the end of each show. Noah was her partner, video editor, and marketing manager, and the two of them made a great team. In fact, they had saved enough money to take a trip to Greece, and they would document the journey on their channel so they would be earning while vacationing.

Parenting While Autistic

While Lucia and Naima were still getting used to the fact that their daughter was neither autistic nor gay, she had been creating her best life, doing what she loved, and making a good living at it. It was a relief to know that she was happy and successful on her own career path and that, even though it looked nothing like what they imagined for her, it was her own. Once she turned eighteen, she was no longer their "job," and they determined to forge a new relationship with their girl as adult equals and friends.

They started by liking and subscribing to her channel.

Maria, Newly Diagnosed Autistic Mom, Empty Nest Update

Faith and Hope finished college and grad school, one earning a degree in school psychology and the other in school counseling. They barely spent any time at home after graduation before they had jobs in neighboring school districts and were ready to be on their own. They went in together to buy a duplex, giving each of them the best of both worlds—being close to their twin while having their independence. Maria was happy that they had become such close friends. She and her own sister had struggled to maintain a relationship long-distance, but it was working better for them now.

Maria wondered sometimes if her girls had become so close to each other because they were twins or because she had been unavailable to them emotionally when they were growing up. She hadn't known she was autistic until they were in college, but she had always been who she was, with or without a diagnosis.

7: Parenting Adults

Finally, she decided that it was a good thing, not a negative reflection on her own parenting skills, that the two girls were so close to each other. She had always done what she thought was best for them, and now she was ready to focus more on herself. Her empty nest was a haven of privacy and serenity.

Robert & Helen, Grandparenting While Autistic, Empty Nest, the Sequel

Robert struggled with the many changes in their family. He had gotten used to having Bobby living with them. To Robert, the way it had always been was the way it should always be. When Bobby and his mom, Lena, moved in with Patrick, the new stepdad, Robert worried they'd never see them again.

He was wrong. Bobby, being autistic himself, also had a strong preference for the familiar, and his grandparents' home was a safe "home base" for him to visit whenever he needed a break from his parents. After their trip to the anime convention during Lena's honeymoon, it became an annual Grandpa-Bobby event that they both looked forward to every year. The convention itself was like a friend that they loved to visit again and again.

After he graduated from high school, Bobby moved back in with Robert and Helen while attending community college. He earned an AA in technology and got an entry-level position as an IT Support Specialist in a fairly small local company, where they valued his attention to detail, one of the features of his autism.

Parenting While Autistic

Eventually, Bobby moved out into a studio apartment of his own, which he decorated with posters and memorabilia from the anime cons. He created a new routine of having dinner with his mom and stepdad every Saturday night and supper with his grandparents every Sunday. Once a month, Lena and Patrick joined them. Robert and Bobby both loved the repetition of doing the same things, eating the same suppers, and sharing the same interests over the years. Some things changed, but the important things, like family, stayed the same, which was just how Robert liked it.

Daisy & Crow, Foster Parents, Not-So-Empty Nest Update

DAISY: *(peers over Kitty's shoulder at her laptop screen)* So, how are your studies going?

KITTY: Still fine. I'll let you know if I need any help.

CROW: If you keep interrupting her studies to ask her how her studies are going, she'll never get anything done.

DAISY: I know. I'm just not used to the idea of online college. Is it real or just a huge scam? Will you get a diploma we can hang on the wall or just some kind of metaphysical NFT thingamabob?

CROW: You worry too much.

DAISY: I can't hang an NFT on the wall, now, can I? I want something fungible!

CROW: It's not your diploma, it's Kitty's.

7: Parenting Adults

DAISY: Kitty, don't you want a nice, fungible diploma on the wall?

KITTY: *(looks up from her computer and blinks)* What?

DAISY: A fungible token.

KITTY: Um, I think I'll just get back to my paper and let you two figure out *(makes vague circular hand motions in their direction)* all this.

CROW: Sorry, Kitty. You keep studying, we'll leave you to it.

KITTY: Thanks. *(goes back to her computer)*

DAISY: *(whispers)* I'm worried about that girl.

KITTY: You know I can hear you.

DAISY: *(whispers)* She can't hear me, I'm whispering.

CROW: *(whispers back)* Everybody can hear you.

DAISY: *(whispers)* Disagree.

CROW: What? Did you say something? I can't hear you. Have I gone deaf? Daisy, speak to me!

DAISY: *(throws a sofa pillow at Crow)*

CROW: *(catches the pillow and laughs)* Come into the kitchen and help me with dinner.

CROW: *(prepares vegetables for stir fry)* I get that you're worried, but I don't know why. You know that once Kitty got help for her reading problem, she did fine in high school. She's responsible and a good student. What is there to worry about?

DAISY: Who's worried? *(chops carrots savagely, knife at arm's length like a broadsword, while pieces of carrot fly around the room)*

Parenting While Autistic

CROW: *(gently takes the knife)* Here, let me take that before you do yourself a mischief. You are a caution with a weapon in your hand.

DAISY: Carrots fear me.

CROW: So do I sometimes. *(they sit at the kitchen table)* Dinner can wait. What's eating you?

DAISY: *(sighs)* Well, Kitty's eighteen now. She's an adult, out of the foster system. So, now that we're not her foster parents, what are we? Maybe she'll leave. I don't want her to leave.

CROW: Neither do I, but if she does find her own place, I'd be happy for her. Wouldn't you? I mean, moving out on your own is an important step in growing up.

DAISY: I just don't want anything to change. I like it with you, and Kitty, and Bugbear, forever and ever. No change. I can't trust change.

CROW: Do you trust me? Do you trust Kitty?

DAISY: Of course, with my life!

CROW: Then you can trust that, even if Kitty were to move out on her own, we will always be family.

DAISY: You're right. You're right. I'm just getting used to it. It makes me itch when I think about Kitty moving out.

CROW: Everything in the universe could change, but I will still be by your side. Forever. Count on it.

DAISY: *(leans her forehead against Crow's)* Yes. I do count on it, every day.

7: Parenting Adults

CROW: Okay then. Do you think you can slice the rest of the carrots without bits flying everywhere?

DAISY: I make no promises. *(holds out her hand)* My sword. Gimme!

As it happened, Kitty completed her online university degree, and she did get a real diploma that Daisy could hang on the wall. The three of them were happy living together, and that didn't change just because Kitty aged out of the foster system and got a job. They were a family, and living together was the perfect decision for them.

PARENT TO PARENT

"I always told the kids that if they ever had a problem or they thought I was doing something different than what they would appreciate me doing, that they should come to me and tell me. They did try this, but they tell me that I didn't always react well, so they stopped. I didn't have the best reaction because it was a change that I couldn't reconcile in a timely manner. Now, I tell my children when they want to tell me something like this, give me twenty-four hours to think about it. Again, I wish I had known then what I know now about autism and about myself.

"Now that I have been diagnosed with autism, I am learning to, as they say, 'go with the flow.' It is very, very difficult for me, but now when I'm with my children I just keep repeating in my head, 'Go with the flow, go with the flow, go with the flow.' They do notice and appreciate my seemingly more relaxed demeanor, even though inside my mind it is not always so relaxed."

— James, late-diagnosed autistic dad

"Being an autistic parent has its own unique challenges, but it also has its own unique strengths! When your child is sad, frightened, or feeling big emotions, you know how deeply those emotions can be felt, and I think this provides a beautiful opportunity for empathy between your child and you."

— Krista, autistic mom

Conclusion

You've Got This!

"All children can flourish and mature through love."
— Ron Sandison, autistic parent, pastor, medical professional,
and author of *A Parent's Guide to Autism*

Conclusion

It is early morning on Mother's Day as I write this last chapter of *Parenting While Autistic*. Later, I will enjoy spending time with my three children, two of them autistic like their dad, and one in the neuro-majority, like me. Our day will probably include laughter, stories, sweet memories, and good food. Throughout the writing of this book, my thoughts have often turned to my late husband, David, remembering our time together with love and gratitude. It was a particular joy to know that he could understand and empathize with all of our children, in a way that might not have been as natural had he not been late-diagnosed autistic himself, as two of our children are.

If you're in the neuro-majority co-parenting with an autistic partner as I did, or if you're a child with an autistic parent, I hope this book has increased your understanding and appreciation for your autistic family member.

If you're parenting while autistic, like my husband and so many other loving and capable parents, I hope you found encouragement and affirmation in these pages. Many of the features of autism, such as loyalty and devotion to family, are important parenting strengths. Other characteristics, such as sensory sensitivities, social preferences, and communication styles, can be managed with understanding, planning, and accommodations. Your lived experience as an autist will be invaluable to you as you parent a new generation of people, whether neurodivergent or neuro-majority.

As you navigate the balance between care for others and self-care, your children will learn that you value them and that you can be counted on to be there for them, along with the message that each of us deserves time for ourselves, even parents.

Especially parents.

When you "put on your own oxygen mask first," as airline staff instruct, by scheduling needed time for de-stressing and recharging, you ensure that you have the capacity to be there for your children. You also teach them that everyone—even parents, even they themselves—everyone is worthy. Advocating for your needs teaches your children how to advocate for their own needs. Taking care of yourself means you will be more actively present to engage with your family, rather than finding yourself overwhelmed.

So create your family calendar to support everyone's needs, whether it's a need for a parent to attend a game or recital, a need for a graceful exit from a social event, or a need for planned recovery time between social activities.

Maria Shriver, mother of four, wrote about parenting, "Having kids—the responsibility of rearing good, kind, ethical, responsible human beings—is the biggest job anyone can embark on. As with any risk, you have to take a leap of faith and ask lots of wonderful people for their help and guidance."

On your personal leap of faith into parenting, I predict you will find wonderful people along your way who will give you the help and guidance you so richly deserve. I also believe that you, yourself,

Conclusion

will be one of those wonderful people offering help and encouragement to others.

Just as "love is love is love," family is family is family. It's not only the people who were born into your family. You can choose whom you let into your family circle. Richard Bach wrote, "The bond that links your true family is not one of blood, but of respect and joy in each other." My wish for everyone reading this is that you find your true family, whether born to you or chosen by you. I hope you accept and return all of the love that is there for you.

In parting, I leave you with these words from Benjamin Spock, legendary parenting expert. Dr. Spock wrote, "Trust yourself. You know more than you think you do."

Believe him, and believe me: You've got this!

PARENT TO PARENT

"I wish I had been diagnosed with autism when I was younger so I could have been given tools for interacting with society. Growing up and raising kids, I knew that I was different, and I knew that I had a challenge with changes. I'm glad that our society today is finally recognizing and learning more and more about brain differences. I think it's a parent's job to allow their kids their feelings and to work them out in their own time. My prayer is that my children will recognize these issues early and accommodate them to make their life an easier one."

— James, late-diagnosed autistic dad

Parenting While Autistic

"The ability of autistics to pick and choose which social norms they want to participate in is a huge advantage in raising children. I have to evaluate almost every social norm before I understand it and decide whether or not it's something I want in my life. Teaching your kids this skill gives them a tremendous advantage in their lives, whether or not they are neurodiverse. Just knowing that you don't have to 'keep up with the Joneses' can be freeing and allow you (and your children) to pursue the life you want."

— Krista, autistic mom

"This is autism. I am still the same person I have always been. Only now I am better because I have more knowledge and understanding of who I am and what I can achieve."
— Lucy Parker, "The Truth About Being Autistic and a Mother"

ACKNOWLEDGMENTS

This book would not be here today without the invaluable support of many people.

- Jennifer Gilpin Yacio, Susan Thompson, and the entire amazing team at Future Horizons, Inc. It is a privilege to work with you!
- Collaborative editor Siobhan Marsh, early reader Cynthia Whitcomb, and autism sensitivity readers Cat David Marsh and Noel Marsh, for making this book much better than it would have been without them.
- My writing family and supportive friends, Susan Fletcher, Diane Hagood, Pamela Smith Hill, Linda Leslie, Kristi Negri, Cherie Walters, Cynthia Whitcomb, Laura Whitcomb. Your encouragement means so much!
- The inspiration and support of my children, Cat, Siobhan, and Noel; my brother, Jonathan Whitcomb, and sisters, Cynthia Whitcomb and Laura Whitcomb, authors all; and the memory of my parents, David and Susanne Whitcomb, who always believed we could achieve whatever we put our minds to; and especially my beloved David Scott Marsh, my dearest example of parenting while autistic.
- I am grateful to the autistic parents who shared so graciously their own inspiring stories of parenting while autistic. Thank you, James. Thank you, Kristi. Your lived experience will shine a light for so many autistic parents and parents-to-be to follow.

RESOURCES

Brazelton, T. Berry, and Joshua D. Sparrow. *TouchPoints: Birth to Three*. Hachette Books, 2021.

Caplan, Frank, and Theresa Caplan. *The First Twelve Months of Life: Your Baby's Growth Month by Month*. Random House Publishing Group, 1995.

DeBellis, Marissa. "A Group Home Exclusively for Married Couples with Developmental Disabilities: A Natural Next-Step." *Touro Law Review* 28, no. 2 (July 18, 2012).

DeWeerdt, Sarah and Spectrum. "The Joys and Challenges of Being a Parent with Autism." *The Atlantic*. https://www.theatlantic.com/family/archive/2017/05/autism-parenting/526989/

Endow, Judy. "Aspects of Autism Translated." http://www.judyendow.com/blog/

Erinphillips84. "Autism and Pregnancy: A Birth Experience." *Neuroclastic*. https://neuroclastic.com/autism-and-birth/

Erwin, Cheryl L., and Jennifer Costa. *The Conscious Parent's Guide to Raising Boys: A Mindful Approach to Raising a Confident, Resilient Son*. Adams Media, 2017.

Hollenberg, Linda. "The Autistic Doula: Navigating the Sensory Challenges of Motherhood." *Reframing Autism*, 2001. https://reframingautism.org.au/the-autistic-doula-navigating-the-sensory-challenges-of-motherhood/

Parenting While Autistic

Jones, Peggy, and Pam Young. *Sidetracked Home Executives*. Warner Books, 1983.

Jones, Peggy, and Pam Young. *Sidetracked Sisters Happiness File*. Warner Books, 2012.

Jones-Cooper, Brittany, and Jacquie Cosgrove. "A Mother with Autism Shares Her Experience Raising Two Sons With the Disorder: We're Here, We Exist." *Yahoo!Life.* https://www.yahoo.com/lifestyle/a-mother-with-autism-shares-her-experience-raising-two-sons-with-the-disorder-were-here-we-exist-130041562

Kim, Cynthia. "Motherhood: Autistic Parenting." Autistic Women and Nonbinary Network (AWN). https://awnnetwork.org/motherhood-autistic-parenting/

Lewis, Laura Foran, Hannah Shirling, Emma Beaudoin, Hannah Sheibner, and Alexa Cestrone. "Exploring the Birth Stories of Women on the Autism Spectrum." *Journal of Obstetric, Gynecologic & Neonatal Nursing* (November 2021). https://doi.org/10.1016/j.jogn.2021.08.099

Marsh, Wendela, and Siobhan Marsh. *Homeschooling, Autism Style*. Future Horizons, 2020.

Marsh, Wendela. *Independent Living with Autism*. Future Horizons, 2020.

Marsh, Wendela. *Dating While Autistic*. Future Horizons, 2023.

Marsh, Wendela. *Relating While Autistic*. Future Horizons, 2023.

Resources

McDonnell, Christina G., and Elizabeth A. DeLucia. "Pregnancy and Parenthood Among Autistic Adults: Implications for Advancing Maternal Health and Parental Well-Being." *Autism in Adulthood* 3, no. 1 (March 18, 2021): 100–115. https://doi.org/10.1089/aut.2020.0046

"Pregnancy and Parenthood Among Autistic Adults: Implications for Advancing Maternal Health and Parental Well-Being." *Autism in Adulthood*, March 2021. https://www.liebertpub.com/doi/full/10.1089/aut.2020.0046

Parker, Lucy. "The Truth about Being Autistic and a Mother." *Motherly*, 2019. https://www.mother.ly/life/the-truth-about-being-autistic-and-a-mother/

Rudy, Lisa Joy. "Autistic Adults as Parents or Guardians: How Autistic Adults Raise Kids." *VeryWell Health*, 2022. https://www.verywellhealth.com/autistic-adults-as-parents-4147325

Sandison, Ron. *A Parent's Guide to Autism: Practical Advice, Biblical Wisdom.* Charisma House, 2016.

Sky, Aria. "Being an Autistic Parent." *The Asperger/Autism Network* (AANE) and "Mamautistic." https://www.aane.org/being-an-autistic-parent/

Vandenberg, Stephanie. "How the Experience of Pregnancy May Differ for Women with Autism." *Neurodiverging*, May 31, 2023. https://www.neurodiverging.com/pregnancy-and-autism-pregnancy-is-different-for-autistic-women/.

Printed in the USA
CPSIA information can be obtained
at www.ICGtesting.com
JSHW021933211123
52296JS00001B/1